MW01070594

SPELLEX®
brand
WORD FINDER

George N. Moore
Richard A. Talbot
G. Willard Woodruff

How to Use This Book

This is a wordbook, a collection of several thousand of the words you will use in writing. Spellex™ Word Finder is a tool for you as a writer. You know what you want to say, know what words you want to use and, like anyone else, you are uncertain about the spelling of some of them. Probably, for your final draft of writing, you will want to check some spellings so your ideas are expressed in the best possible form.

Spellex® Word Finder is designed very simply. Over 3000 entry or base words are listed alphabetically. Beside each entry word are several other forms of the word. For example:

pass   passes, passed, passing, passer, passable, past, passage, passenger

Spellex® Word Finder is a very handy, quick word finder. It's meant to do only one thing for you: to provide you, the writer, with a quick way to check on the spelling of a word.

Printed in USA
© 1975—Curriculum Associates, Inc.
Woburn, Mass. 01801
All Rights Reserved
ISBN 0—89187—133—0
10   9   8   7

abandon abandons, abandoned, abandoning

able ability, abilities, ably, ablest

aboard

about

above

abroad

absent absence, absences, absentee, absently

absurd absurdly, absurdity

academy academic, academies

accent accents, accented, accenting

accept accepts, accepted, accepting, acceptance, acceptable, acceptably

accident accidental, accidentally, accidents

accompany accompanies, accompanying, accompanied, accompanist

accomplish accomplishes, accomplishing, accomplished, accomplishment

account accounts, accounted, accounting, accountant, accountable

accurate accurately, accurateness, accuracy

accuse accuses, accused, accusing, accuser, accusation

accustom accustomed, accustoms

ache aches, ached, aching

acid acidly, acidity

acknowledge acknowledges, acknowledged, acknowledging, acknowledgeable, acknowledgement

acquaint

acquaint   acquaintance, acquaintances, acquaints, acquainted, acquainting

acquire   acquired, acquires, acquiring, acquisition

acre   acres, acreage

across

act   acts, acted, acting

action   actions

active   actively, activeness, activity, activities

actor   actress

add   adds, adding, addend, addition, additional, additionally, additions, additive, added

address   addresses, addressed, addressing, addressee

administration   administrations, administrate, administrative, administrator

admire   admires, admired, admiring, admiration, admirer, admirable

admit   admits, admitted, admitting, admittedly, admittance, admission

adopt   adopts, adopted, adopting, adoptable, adoption

advance   advanced, advances, advancing, advancement

advantage   advantages, advantageous

adventure   adventures, adventured, adventuring, adventurous, adventurer, adventuresome

advertise   advertises, advertised, advertising, advertiser, advertisement

advise   advice, advises, advised, advising, advisor

affair   affairs

affect   affects, affected, affecting, affective, affectedly, affectedness, affectionate, affectionately, affection, affections

afford   affords, afforded, affording

afraid

after   afterward

afternoon   afternoons

again

against

age   ages, aged, ageless, aging

agent   agents, agency, agencies

ago

agree   agrees, agreed, agreeing, agreeable, agreeably, agreement

agriculture   agricultural, agriculturally, agriculturist

ah

ahead

aid   aids, aided, aiding

aim   aims, aimed, aiming, aimless, aimlessness

air   airy

airplane   airpianes, aircraft

airport   airports

aisle   aisles

alarm   alarms, alarmed, alarming, alarmingly, alarmist

alike   like, likeness

alive   live, lives, lived, living, lively

all

all

alley   alleys, alleyway

allow   allowed, allowing, allowable,
allowance

all right   all wrong

almost

alone

along

already

also

although

altogether

always

A.M.

ambition   ambitions, ambitious,
ambitiously

ambulance

amendment   amendments, amend,
amends, amended, amending

American   Americans, America

ammunition   ammunitions

among   amongst

amount   amounts, amounted,
amounting

amuse   amuses, amused, amusing,
amusement

an

analyze   analyzes, analyzed,
analyzing, analytical, analyst,
analysis

ancestor   ancestors, ancestress,
ancestral, ancestry

anchor   anchors, anchored, anchoring, anchorage

ancient   anciently, ancientness

and

anger   angers, angered, angering, angry, angrily, angrier, angriest

angle   angles, angled, angling

animal   animals

animate   animated, animation

anniversary   anniversaries

announce   announces, announced, announcing, announcement, announcer

annual   annually, annuals

another

answer   answers, answered, answering

ant   ants, anthill

anteater

anticipate   anticipates, anticipated, anticipating, anticipation

anxious   anxiousness, anxiously, anxiety, anxieties

any   anyone, anybody, anyhow, anyplace, anything, anyway, anywhere, anytime, anymore

apart

apiece   piece, pieces, pieced, piecing

apologize   apologizes, apologized, apologizing, apology, apologies

appear   appears, appeared, appearing, appearance

appetite   appetites, appetizer, appetizing

apple   apples

applesauce

apply   applies, applied, applying, applicable, application, applicant, applier, applicator

appointment   appoint, appoints, appointed, appointing

appreciation   appreciate, appreciates, appreciated, appreciating, appreciable, appreciably, appreciative

approach   approaches, approached, approaching, approachable

approve   approves, approved, approving, approval, approvingly

April   Apr.

apron   aprons

are   aren't

area   areas

argument   arguments, argue, argues, argued, arguing, argumentative

arise   arises, arose, arising, arisen

arithmetic   arithmetically

arm   arms, armless, armed, arming, armor, armored, armory, armament

army   armies

arose   arise, arising, arises

around

arrange   arranges, arranged, arranging, arrangement

arrest   arrests, arresting, arrested

arrive   arrives, arrived, arriving, arrival

art   arts, artist, artistic, artists, artful, artfully, artisan, artistically, artless, artlessly

article articles

artificial artificially

as

ash ashes, ashen, ashy

aside asides

ask asked, asking, asks

asleep sleep, sleeps, slept, sleeping, sleepy, sleepless, sleeper

assembly assemblies, assemble, assembles, assembled, assembling

assign assignment, assignments, assigns, assigned, assigning

assist assistance, assists, assisted, assisting, assistant

association associations, associate, associates, associated, associating

assure assures, assured, assuring, assurance, assuredly

astonish astonished, astonishes, astonishing, astonishment, astonishingly

at

athlete athletes, athletic, athletics, athletically

attack attacks, attacked, attacking, attacker

attempt attempts, attempted, attempting

attend attends, attended, attending, attendance, attention, attentive, attentively, attendant

attic attics

attitude attitudes

attorney attorneys

attract

attract   attracts, attracted, attracting, attractive, attraction, attractively, attractiveness

auction   auctions, auctioneer, auctioned, auctioning

August   Aug.

aunt   aunts

author   authors, authored, authoring, authoress

authority   authorities, authoritative, authorize

automation   automatic, automated

automobile   auto, autos, automobiles, automotive

autumn

available   availability, availably, availableness, avail

avenue   avenues, ave.

average   averages, averaged, averaging, av.

aviation   aviator, aviatrix

avoid   avoids, avoided, avoiding, avoidable, avoidably, avoidance

await   awaits, awaited, awaiting

awake   awakened, awakes, awaking, awoke, awaken, awaked, awakening

awe   awed

awful   awfully

awkward   awkwardly, awkwardness

awl   awls

ax   axe, axes, axing, axed

axle   axles, axis

baby   babies, babe, babied, babyish, babying

bachelor   bachelors, bachelorhood

back   backs, backing, backed, backer

bad   badly, badness

badge   badges

bag   bags, bagged, bagging, bagger

bait   baits, baited, baiting, baiter

bake   bakery, bakeries, bakes, baked, baking, baker

balance   balances, balanced, balancing

bale   bales, baler, baled, baling

ball   balls, balled, balling, balloon

ballet   ballets, ballerina

ballot   ballots, balloted, balloting

banana   bananas

band   bands, banding, banded, bandage, bandages, bandaged, bandaging

bang   bangs, banged, banging

banister   banisters

bank   banks, banker, banked, banking

banquet   banquets, banqueted, banqueting

bar   bars, barring, barred

bare   bares, bareheaded, barehanded, barely, baring, bared, barelegged, barefaced

bargain   bargains, bargained, bargaining, bargainer

bark   barks, barker, barking, barked

barn   barns, barnlike

barrel   barrels, barreled, barreling, barrelful

base   bases, based, basing, basic, basement, basements

baseball

basket   baskets, basketball

bathe   bathes, bathed, bathing, bather, bath

bathroom   bathrooms

battery   batteries

battle   battles, battling

bay   bays, bayed, baying

be   been, being

beach   beaching, beaches, beached

bead   beads, beading, beaded, beady

beam   beams, beamed, beaming

bean   beans, beanie

bear   bears, bearing, bearable, bore, borne

beard   bearded, beardless, beards, bearding

beast   beasts, beastly, beastlike

beat   beaten, beats, beating, beater

beautiful   beautifully, beauty, beautify, beautifies, beautified, beautifying

beaver   beavers

because

become   becomes, becoming, becomingly, became

bed   beds, bedding, bedded

bedroom   bedrooms

bedtime   bedtimes

bee   bees, beehive, beeline

beef   beefy

beet   beets

before

beg   begs, begged, begging, beggar, beggars, beggarly

begin   began, beginning, begun, beginner, begins

behalf

behave   behaves, behaved, behaving, behavior

behind

believe   believes, believer, believing, believed, belief, believable

bell   bells, belled, belling

belong   belongs, belonged, belonging

belove   beloved

below

belt   belted, belts, belting, beltway

beneath

bench   benches, benching, benched

bend   bends, bending, bent, bendable

benefits   benefit, benefited, benefiting, beneficiary, beneficial

berry   berries, berried, berrying

berth   berths

beside   besides

best   better

bet   bets, betted, betting, bettor

between

beyond

Bible

Bible   Bibles, biblical

bicycle   bicycles, bicycling, bicycled, bicyclist

bid   bids, bidding, bidder

big   bigger, biggest, bigness

bike   bikes, biked, biking

bill   bills, billed, billing

bind   binds, binding, bound, boundless

bird   birds, birdlike, birdhouse, birdseed, birdcage, birdcall

birth   births, born

birthday   birthdays

biscuit   biscuits

bite   biting, bites, bitten, bit

biweekly   weekly, week

black   blacks, blacken, blackening, blacker, blackest, blackened

blackberry   blackberries

blade   blades

blame   blames, blamed, blaming, blameless

blanket   blankets, blanketed, blanketing

blast   blasted, blasting, blasts

blaze   blazes, blazed, blazing, blazer

blind   blinding, blinded, blinds

block   blocks, blocking, blocker

blood   bleed, bleeds, bleeding, bled, bloody, bloodiest, bloodier

blossom   blossoms, blossomed, blossoming

blouse   blouses

blow   blew, blows, blowing, blower, blown, blowy

blue   bluer, bluest, blues, bluing

blueberry   blueberries

bluff   bluffs, bluffed, bluffing, bluffer

board   boards, boarded, boarding, boarder

boat   boating, boats, boated

body   bodies, bodily

boil   boiler, boilers, boils, boiled, boiling

bomb   bombs, bomber, bombed

bond   bonds, bonder, bonded, bondage

bone   bones, bony, boned

bonnet   bonnets

boo   boos

book   books, booked, bookish, booking, booklet

bookcase   bookcases

border   borders, bordered, bordering

bore   boring, bored, bores, boredom

born   bear, bearing, bore, birth

borrow   borrows, borrowed, borrowing, borrower

boss   bossing, bossed, bossy

both

bother   bothers, bothered, bothering

bottle   bottles, bottling, bottled, bottler

bottom   bottoms

bough

bough   boughs

boulevard   boulevards

bound   boundary, bounds, bounded,
bounding, boundless, bounder, bind

bow   bows, bowed, bowing, bower

bowl   bowls, bowled, bowler, bowling

box   boxes, boxing, boxed, boxer

boy   boys, boyhood, boyish

brain   brains, brainy, brainless,
braininess, brainlessly

brake   brakes, braked, braking

branch   branches, branched,
branching

brass   brasses, brassy, brassier,
brassiest

brave   bravely, bravery

bread   breads, breadlike,
breadbasket

break   breaks, broke, broken,
breaking, breaker

breakfast   breakfasts

breast   breasts, breasted

breath   breathless, breathlessly,
breathlessness

breathe   breathes, breathed,
breathing, breather

breeze   breezy, breezeway

briar   briars

bridge   bridges, bridged, bridging

brief   briefly, briefer, briefest, brevity,
briefness

bright   brighter, brightest, brightly,
brightness, brighten, brightens,
brightened, brightening, brightener

brilliant   brilliantly, brilliance

bring   brings, brought, bringing

brisk   brisker, briskest, briskly, briskness

broad   broadly, broader, broadest, broaden, broadening

brook   brooks, brooklet

brother   brothers, brotherly

brought   bring, bringing

brown   browns, browned, browning, browner, brownest

bruise   bruises, bruised, bruising, bruisingly

brush   brushes, brushed, brushing

bubble   bubbling, bubbles, bubbled

bucket   buckets

buffalo   buffaloes

bug   bugs, bugged, bugging

bugle   bugles, bugled, bugling, bugler

build   built, builds, building, builder, buildings

bull   bulls, bulled, bully

bulldog   bulldogs

bullet   bullets

bullpen   bullpens

bully   bullies, bullied, bullying

bump   bumper, bumpers, bumps, bumped, bumping, bumpy

bunch   bunches, bunched, bunching

bundle   bundles, bundled, bundling

bunk   bunks, bunking, bunkhouse, bunkbed

bunny   bunnies

burden   burdens, burdened,
burdening, burdensome

burglar   burglars, burglary, burglaries

burn   burns, burned, burning, burner

burst   bursting, bursts

bury   burial, buried, buries, burying

bus   buses or busses, busing

bush   bushes, bushiest, bushier,
bushy

bushel   bushels

bust   busts, busted, busting

busy   business, businesses, busier,
busiest, busying, busybody, busied

but   buts

butcher   butchers, butchering

butter   buttered, butters, buttery,
buttering

butterfly   butterflies

button   buttons, buttoned, buttoning,
buttonhole

buy   buys, buying, bought, buyer

by   bypass, bygone, byproduct,
bypath, bye

cabbage   cabbages

cabin   cabins

cabinet   cabinets, cabinetmaker

cable   cables, cabled, cabling

cage   cages, caged, caging

cake   cakes, caked, caking

calf   calves, calving, calved

call   calling, calls, called, caller

calm   calmly, calms, calming, calmed, calmer, calmest, calmness

camp   camps, camped, camper, campers, camping

campaign   campaigns, campaigned, campaigning, campaigner

campus   campuses

can   cans, canned, canning, cannery

canal   canals

candidate   candidates, candidacy

candy   candies, candied, candying

cane   canes, caned, caning

canoe   canoes, canoeing, canoed

can't   cannot

cap   caps, capped, capping

capable   capably, capability, capabilities

capacity   capacities

capital   capitals, capitalize, capitalized, capitalizing

captain   captains, captained

capture   captures, captured, capturing, captor, captivate, captive, captivity

car   cars

card   cards

cardboard

care

care   cares, cared, caring, careless, carelessness, careful, carefully, carefulness

career   careers

cargo   cargoes

carpet   carpets, carpeted, carpeting

carrot   carrots

carry   carried, carries, carrying, carrier, carriage

cart   carts, carted, carting

case   cases, cased, casing, casement

cash   cashes, cashed, cashing, cashier

cast   casting, castaway

castle   castles

cat   cats, catty

catalog   catalogs, cataloger, catalogist, catalogued

catch   catches, catcher, catching, caught

cattle   cattleman, cattlemen

cause   causes, caused, causing

caution   cautiously, cautious, cautiousness, cautionary, cautioning, cautions, cautioned

cave   caves

ceiling   ceilings

celebrate   celebrates, celebrated, celebrating, celebration, celebrity, celebrities

cell   cells

cellar   cellars

cement   cements, cemented, cementing

cemetery   cemeteries

cent   cents

cent   centimeter, centipede

center   centers, centered, centering, central, centrally

century   centuries

cereal   cereals

certain   certainly, certainty

certify   certificate, certificates, certification, certifies, certified, certifying

chain   chains, chained, chaining

chair   chairs

chairman   chairmen, chairwoman, chairwomen, chairperson

chalk   chalks, chalked, chalking

chamber   chambers

champion   champions, championed, championship, championships, championing

chance   chances, chanced, chancing

change   changes, changed, changing changeable, changeless

channel   channels, channeled, channeling

chapel   chapels

chapter   chapters

character   characters, characteristic, characteristics, characteristically

charge   charges, charged, charging, charger

charity   charities, charitable, charitably, charitableness

charm

charm charms, charmed, charming, charmer, charmingly

chase chased, chasing, chases

chauffeur chauffeurs, chauffeured, chauffeuring

cheap cheaper, cheapest, cheaply, cheapness

cheat cheats, cheated, cheating, cheater

check checks, checked, checker, checking

cheek cheeks, cheekbone

cheer cheers, cheered, cheering, cheerful, cheerfully, cheery, cheerier, cheeriest, cheerlessly, cheerleader

cheese cheeses, cheesy

cherry cherries

chest chests

chew chews, chewed, chewing, chewy

chick chicks, chicken, chickens

chief chiefs, chiefly, chieftain

child children, childish, childishly, childlike

chin chins, chinned, chinning

chocolate chocolates

choir choirs

choose chose, chooses, choosing, chosen, choice, choices, choosy, choosier, choosiest, choosiness, choiceness

chop chops, chopped, chopping, chopper, choppy, choppier, choppiest

chorus choruses, chorused, chorusing, choral

Christmas

church   churches

cigar   cigars, cigarette, cigarettes

circle   circles, circled, circling,
   circular, cycle

circulation   circulative, circulatory,
   circulate, circulates, circulated,
   circulating, circulator

circus   circuses

citizen   citizens, citizenship

city   cities

civil   civilly, civilian, civilize, civilized,
   civilizing, civilization, civilizations

claim   claims, claimed, claiming,
   claimable, claimer, claimant

class   classes, classy, classical,
   classify, classified, classifier,
   classification, classifications,
   classed, classless, classroom,
   classmate

clay   clays

clean   cleans, cleaned, cleaning,
   cleaner, cleanest, cleanly
   cleanliness, cleanable, cleanse

clear   clearer, clearest, clearly,
   clearness, clears, cleared, clearing,
   clearance

clerk   clerks, clerked, clerking

clever   cleverly, cleverness, cleverer,
   cleverest

cliff   cliffs

climate   climates, climatic

climb   climbs, climbed, climbing,
   climber

cloak   cloaks, cloaked, cloaking

clock   clocks, clocked, clocking

close

close   closely, closer, closest, closed, closing, closes

closet   closets, closeted

cloth   cloths, clothe, clothes, clothing, clothed

cloud   clouds, cloudy, clouded, clouding, cloudier, cloudiest, cloudless

clown   clowns, clowned, clowning, clownish

club   clubs, clubbed, clubbing, clubhouse

coach   coaches, coached, coaching

coal   coals

coarse   coarser, coarsest, coarseness, coarsely

coast   coasts, coasted, coasting, coaster, coastal

coat   coats, coated, coating

cocoa

coffee   coffeepot

coin   coins, coined, coining, coinage

cold   colds, colder, coldest, coldness, cool

collar   collars, collared, collaring

collect   collects, collected, collecting, collection, collections, collectable, collector

college   colleges, collegiate, collegian

colonel   colonels

colony   colonies, colonial, colonist, colonize, colonized, colonizing, colonization

color   colors, coloring, colored, colorful, colorfully

colt colts, coltish

column columns, columnist, columned

comb combs, combed, combing, comblike, comber

come comes, coming, came

comet comets

comfort comforts, comforted, comforting, comfortable, comfortably, comforter

command commands, commanded, commanding, commander, commandment, commandingly

commence commences, commenced, commencement, commencing

commerce commercial, commercially, commercialism

commission commissions, commissioned, commissioning, commissioner

commit commits, committing, committedly

committee committees, committeeman, committeemen, commit, committeeperson

common commons, commoner, commonest, commonly

communicate communication, communications, communicated, communicating, communicator

community communities, commune, communal, communism

companion companions, companionable, companionship, companionless

company companies

compare

compare   comparative, comparatively, comparison, comparable, compares, compared, comparing

compete   competition, competitive, competitor, competed, competing, competes

complete   completes, completed, completing, completion, completeness, completely

compose   composes, composed, composing, composition, compositions, composer

concern   concerns, concerned, concerning, concernment

concert   concerts

conclude   conclusion, conclusions, concludes, concluding, concluded, conclusive, conclusively

concrete   concretes, concreteness, concretely

condition   conditioned, conditioning, conditional, conditions

conduct   conducts, conducted, conducting, conductor, conduction

confer   confers, conferring, conferred, conference, conferences

confine   confined, confines, confining, confineable, confinement

confirm   confirmation, confirmed, confirming

conform   conformity, conforms, conformed, conforming

confuse   confuses, confused, confusing, confusion, confusingly

congress   congressional, congressman

connect   connects, connected, connecting, connection, connector

conquer conquers, conquered, conquering, conqueror, conquest

consent consents, consented, consenting

consider considers, considered, considering, considerable, considerate, consideration, considerations, considerately

constant constantly

constitution constitute, constitutes, constituted, constituting, constitutions, constitutional, constitutionally

construct constructs, constructing, constructed, constructive, constructively, construction

consult consults, consulted, consulting, consultant, consultation

contact contacts, contacted, contacting

contain contains, contained, containing, container

content contents, contented, contentment, contentedly

contest contests, contested, contesting, contestants

continue continues, continued, continuing, continuation, continuous, continuously, continual, continually, continuity

contract contracts, contracted, contracting, contractual, contraction,contractor

contrary contrarily, contrariness

control controls, controlled, controlling, controller

convene convenes, convened, convening, convention, conventions, conventional, conventionally

convenient   conveniently, convenience, conveniences, convenienced

converse   conversed, conversing, conversation, conversations

cook   cooks, cooked,cooking, cookout, cookbook

cookie   cookies

cool   cooler, coolest, cooling, coolness, cools, cooled, coolly

cooperate   cooperates, cooperated, cooperating, cooperation, cooperative, cooperatively, cooperativeness

copy   copies, copied, copying, copier

copper   coppered, coppery

corn   corncob, cornhusk, cornstalk, cornstarch, cornmeal

corner   corners, cornered, cornering, cornerstone

correct   corrects, corrected, correcting, correction, correctional, correctly, correctness, corrective

correspond   corresponds, corresponded, corresponding, correspondence

cost   costs, costing, costly

costume   costumes, costumed, costuming

cottage   cottages

cotton   cottons, cottontail

cough   coughs, coughed, coughing

could   couldn't

council   councils, councilor, councilman, councilwoman, councilors

count   counts, counted, counting, counter

country   countries

county   counties

couple   couples, coupling, coupled

courage   courageous, courageously, courageousness

course   courses

court   courts, courted, courting

courtesy   courtesies, courteous, courteously

cousin   cousins

cover   covers, covered, covering, coverage, coveralls

cow   cows, cowbell, cowbird, cowboy, cowboys

crack   cracks, cracked, cracking, crackle

cracker   crackers

crash   crashed, crashes, crashing

crawl   crawls, crawled, crawling, crawler

craze   crazy, crazed, crazier, craziest, crazily, craziness

creak   creaks, creaking, creaked

cream   creams, creamed, creamier, creamy

create   creates, creating, creator, creation

creature   creatures

credit   credits, credited, crediting, creditor

creek   creeks

creep   creeping, creeps, crept

crew   crews

crime   crimes, criminal, criminally

crook

crook   crooked, crooks

crop   crops, cropped, cropping

cross   crosses, crossed, crossing, crossly, crosswalk, crosscheck, crossfire, crossover, crossroad

crouch   crouches, crouched, crouching

crow   crows, crowed, crowing

crowd   crowds, crowded, crowding

cruel   crueler, cruelest, cruelly, cruelty, cruelness

crush   crushes, crushed, crushing, crusher

cry   cries, cried, crying, crier

crystal   crystals, crystalize, crystalizes, crystalized

cucumber   cucumbers

cultivate   cultivates, cultivated, cultivating, cultivator, cultivation

cunning   cunningly

cup   cups, cupful, cupsful, cupped, cupping, cupboard, cupcake

curious   curiously, curiosity, curio

current   currents, currently

curtain   curtains

curve   curves, curved, curving

cushion   cushions, cushioned, cushioning

custom   customs, customary

customer   customers

cut   cuts, cutting, cutter, cutoff, cutout, cutup

cute   cuter, cutest, cuteness, cutely

dad dads, daddy

dairy dairies, dairyman, dairymaid

daisy daisies

dam dams, dammed, damming

damage damages, damaged, damaging

dance dances, danced, dancing, dancer

danger dangers, dangerous, dangerously

dare dares, dared, daring, daringly, darer

dark darker, darkest, darkish, darkening, darken, darkened

darling darlings

dash dashed, dashing, dashes

date dates, dated, dating, dateline

daughter daughters

dawn dawns, dawned, dawning

day days, daily, daybreak, daydream, daylight, daytime

dead deadly, deadlier, deadliest, die, died, death, deathly, deadline

deaf deafen, deafens, deafened, deafening

deal deals, dealt, dealing, dealer

dear dearer, dearest

debate debates, debated, debating, debater

debt debts, debtor

decade decades

December Dec.

decent decently, decency

deceive deceives, deceived, deceiving, deceit, deceitful, deceiver

decide decides, decided, deciding, decidedly

decision decisions, decisive, decisively

deck decks, decked, decking

declare declares, declared, declaring, declaration

decline declines, declined, declining

decorate decorates, decorated, decorating, decoration, decorative, decorator

deed deeds

deep deeper, deepest, deeply, deepen, deepening, deepened

deer deers, deerskin

defeat defeats, defeated, defeating

defend defends, defended, defending, defender, defendent, defense, defensively

define defines, defined, defining, definition, definitions

delay delays, delayed, delaying

delicate delicately, delicacy, delicacies

delicious deliciously

delight delights, delighted, delighting, delightful, delightfully

deliver delivers, delivered, delivering, delivery

demand demands, demanded, demanding

democrat democrats, democratic, democracy, democracies

dent dents, dented, denting

dentist   dentists, dental, dentistry

deny   denies, denied, denying, denial

depart   departs, departed, departing, departure

department   departments, departmental

depend   depends, depended, depending, dependent

deposit   deposits, deposited, depositing, depositor

depot   depots

depth   depths

describe   describes, described, describing, descriptive, descriptively, description, descriptions

desert   deserts, deserted, deserting, deserter

deserve   deserves, deserved, deserving

desire   desires, desired, desiring, desirable, desirability, desirous

desk   desks

despair   despairs, despaired, despairing, despairingly

desperate   desperately, desperateness, desperation, desperado

dessert   desserts

destine   destines, destined, destiny, destination, destinations

destroy   destroys, destroyed, destroying, destroyer, destruction

determine   determines, determined, determining, determination

develop   develops, developed, developing, developer, development

diamond   diamonds

did   didn't

die   died, dies, dying

diet   diets, dieted, dieting, dieter, dietary, dietetic, dietician

differ   differs, differed, differing, difference, different, differently, differentiate

difficult   difficulty, difficulties

dig   digs, digging, digger, dug

digest   digests, digested, digesting, digestible, digestion, digestive

dim   dimly, dimness, dimmer, dimmest, dims, dimmed, dimming

dime   dimes

dine   dinner, dinners, dinnerware, dines, dined, dining

dinosaur   dinosaurs

diploma   diplomas

direct   directs, directed, directing, director, direction, directly

dirty   dirt, dirties, dirtier, dirtiest, dirtied, dirtying

disappear   disappears, disappeared, disappearing, disappearance

disappoint   disappointed, disappoints, disappointment, disappointing

disaster   disasters, disastrous, disastrously

discover   discovers, discovered, discovering, discoverer, discovery

discuss   discusses, discussed, discussing, discussion

disease   diseases, diseased

disgrace   disgraces, disgraced, disgracing, disgraceful, disgracefully

dish   dishes, dished, dishing, dishcloth, dishwasher

dislike   dislikes, disliked, disliking

dismiss   dismisses, dismissed, dismissing, dismissal

displease   displeases, displeased, displeasing, displeasure

dispose   disposes, disposed, disposition, disposing, disposal, disposable

dispute   disputes, disputed, disputing, disputable

distant   distantly, distance

distinct   distinctly, distinction, distinctive, distinctively, distinctiveness

district   districts, districted, districting

ditch   ditches, ditched, ditching

dive   dives, diving, diver, dove

divide   divides, divided, dividing, divider, division, divisible, dividend

do   doing, did, done, does, doesn't, don't

dock   docks, docking, docked, dockyard

doctor   doctors, doctored, doctoring, doctoral, doctorate, Dr.

document   documents, documentary

dog   dogs, doggy, dogged, dogcatcher

doll   dolls, dolled, dolling, doll-like

dollar   dollars

domestic   domestically, domesticate, domestication

donkey

donkey   donkeys

door   doors, doorbell, doorknob, doorway, doorstep

dose   doses, dosed, dosing, dosage

double   doubles, doubled, doubling, doubly

doubt   doubts, doubted, doubting, doubtful, doubtless

down   downs, downy, downed, downing, downhill, downstairs, downtown, downpour

dozen   dozens

drag   drags, dragged, dragging

dragon   dragons, dragonfly

draw   drew, draws, drawing, drawn, drawer, drawings

dream   dreams, dreamed, dreaming, dreamy, dreamless, dreamland

dress   dresses, dresser, dressers, dressed, dressing

drill   drills, drilled, drilling

drink   drank, drinking, drunk, drinks, drinker, drunkard, drunken, drunkenly

drive   driver, drivers, driving, drove, driven, drives, driveway

drop   drops, dropped, dropper, dropping, droplet, dropout

drown   drowns, drowned, drowning

drug   drugs, druggist, drugged, drugging

drum   drums, drummed, drumming, drummer, drumbeat, drumstick

dry   driest, dries, drier, drying

duck   ducks, ducked, ducking, duckling

due   dues

dull   duller, dullest

dumb   dumber, dumbest, dumbbell

during   duration, durable

dust   dusts, dusted, dusting, duster, dusty, dustier, dustiest

duty   duties, dutiful, dutifully

dwarf   dwarfs, dwarfed, dwarfing

each

eager   eagerly, eagerness,

ear   ears, earful, earache, eardrum, earring

early   earlier, earliest

earn   earned, earning, earns

earth   earthen, earthquake, earthworm

east   eastern, easterly, easterner, eastward

Easter

easy   easier, easiest, easily, easygoing

eat   eats, ate, eating, eaten, edible

echo   echoes, echoed, echoing

economy   economical, economically, economics, economize, economist, economic

edge   edges, edged, edging, edger, edgy

edit

edit   edits, edited, editing, editor

editor   editors, editorial, editorially

educate   education, educations, educational, educates, educated, educating, educator

effect   effects, effected, effecting, effective, effectively, effectiveness, effectual

effort   efforts, effortless, effortlessly

egg   eggs, egged, egging, eggbeater, eggshell

eight   eights, eighth, eighteen, eighty

either

elaborate   elaborately, elaborateness, elaborates, elaborated, elaborating, elaborative, elaboration

elect   election, elects, elected, electing, elector, elective, electoral

electric   electricity, electrically, electrical, electrician

elephant   elephants

elevate   elevator, elevators, elevates, elevated, elevating, elevation

eleven   elevens, eleventh

elf   elves, elfish, elfin, elflike

else

embarrass   embarrassment, embarrasses, embarrassing, embarrassed, embarrassingly

embroider   embroiders, embroidered, embroidering, embroidery, embroideries

empire   empires, emperor, empress

empty   empties, emptied, emptying

encourage   encourages, encouraged, encouraging, encouragement

38

end   endless, ends, ended, ending, endlessly

endure   endures, endured, enduring, enduringly, endurable, endurance

enemy   enemies

enforce   enforces, enforced, enforcing, enforcement, enforcer, enforceable

engage   engages, engaged, engaging, engagement

engine   engines, engineer, engineering, engineers, engineered

England   English, New England

enjoy   enjoys, enjoyed, enjoying, enjoyment, enjoyable

enormous   enormously, enormousness, enormity

enough

enter   enters, entered, entering, entrance

entertain   entertains, entertained, entertaining, entertainment, entertainer

entire   entirely, entirety

envelope   envelopes, enveloped, enveloping

equal   equally, equality, equals, equalled, equalling, equate, equating

equip   equipment, equipped, equipping

erase   erases, erased, erasing, eraser

erect   erects, erected, erecting, erection

errand   errands

error   errors, err, errs, erroneous, erroneously, erring

escape escapes, escaped, escaping, escapade

especially special

essay essays, essayist

essence essences, essential, essentially, essentials

establish establishes, established, establishing, establishment

estate estates

estimate estimates, estimated, estimating, estimation

evaporate evaporates, evaporated, evaporating, evaporation, evaporator

eve eves, evening

even evens, evened, evening, evenly

event events, eventful, eventfully, eventfulness, eventually, eventual

ever evergreen, everlasting

every everyone, everything, everywhere, everybody, everyday, everyplace

evidence evidences, evidenced, evidencing, evident, evidently

evil evils, evilly, evilness

exact exacts, exacted, exacting, exactly, exactness

examine examines, examined, examining, examiner, examination

example examples, exemplary, exemplify, exemplifies, exemplifying, exemplified

exceed exceeds, exceeded, exceeding, exceedingly

excel excels, excelled, excelling, excellent, excellence, excellently

except exception, exceptions,
exceptional, exceptionally,
excepting, excepted

excess excesses, excessive,
excessively

exchange exchanges, exchanged,
exchanging

excite excites, excited, exciting,
excitedly, excitingly, excitement

exclaim exclaims, exclaimed,
exclaiming, exclamation,
exclamatory

excuse excuses, excused, excusing

execute executive, executives,
executes, executed, executing

exercise exercises, exercised,
exercising, exerciser

exhibit exhibits, exhibited, exhibiting,
exhibitor, exhibition

exist existence, existences, exists,
existed, existing

expect expects, expected, expecting,
expectation, expectedly

expense expenses, expensive,
expensively, expensiveness

experience experiences,
experienced, experiencing,
experiential

experiment experimental,
experimentation, experimented,
experimenting

expert experts, expertly, expertness,
expertise

explain explains, explained,
explaining, explanation

explode explodes, exploded,
exploding, explosion, explosive,
explosively

explore

explore explores, explored, exploring, exploration, explorer

export exports, exported, exporting, exporter

expose exposure, exposures, exposes, exposed, exposing

express expresses, expressed, expressing, expressly, expression, expressionless, expressive, expressively

extent extensive, extensively, extends, extend, extended, extending

extra extras

extreme extremely, extremism, extremist, extremity

eye eyes, eyed, eyeing, eyeful, eyebrow, eyelash, eyelid, eyeball, eyedropper, eyesight, eyewitness

face faced, faces, facing, facial

fact facts, factual, factually

factory factories

fail fails, failed, failing, failure

fair fairs, fairly, fairer, fairest, fairness, fairground

fairy fairies, fairylike

fall falls, fell, falling, fallen

false falsely, falseness, falsify, falsifies, falsified, falsifying, falsification

fame famous

familiar familiarly, familiarity, familiarities, familiarize, familiarizes, familiarized, familiarizing

family families

fan fans, fanned, fanning

fancy fancier, fanciest, fanciness, fancies, fancied, fancying, fanciful

far farther, farthest

fare fares, fared, faring

farewell farewells

farm farms, farmer, farmers, farmed, farming, farmhouse, farmyard

fashion fashions, fashionable, fashionably, fashioned, fashioning

fast faster, fastest, fasts, fasted, fasting

fasten fastens, fastened, fastening, fastener

fat fatter, fattest, fatten, fattened, fattening, fatty, fattier, fattiest

fatal fatally, fatality

fate fated, fates, fateful, fatefully, fatefulness

father fathers, fathered, fatherly

fault faults, faulted, faulting, faultless, faultlessly, faultlessness, faulty

favor favors, favored, favoring, favorite, favorable, favorably

fear fears, feared, fearing, fearless, fearful, fearfully, fearlessly, fright

feast feasts, feasted, feasting, festive, festivity, festivities, festival

feather feathers, feathered, feathering, feathery

feature features, featured, featuring, featureless

February

February   Feb.

federal   federally, federalize, federation

feeble   feebly, feebleness, feebler, feeblest

feed   feeds, fed, feeding, food

feel   feels, felt, feeling, feelings, feeler

feet   foot, ft.

fellow   fellows, fellowship

female   feminine, femininely, femininity, feminism, feminist

fence   fences, fenced, fencing, fencer

fern   ferns, fernlike

ferry   ferries, ferried, ferrying

fever   fevers, fevered, feverish, feverishly

few   fewer, fewest

fiber   fibers, fibered, fibrous

field   fields, fielding, fielded, fielder

fierce   fiercer, fiercest, fiercely, fierceness

fight   fights, fought, fighting, fighter

figure   figures, figured, figuring, figurative, figuratively

file   files, filed, filing, filer

fill   fills, filled, filling, filler, full

film   films, filmed, filming, filmstrip, filmy

final   finally, finality, finalist

find   finds, finding, finder, found

fine   fines, fined, fining, finer, finest, finely, finery

finger   fingers, fingered, fingering

finish   finishes, finished, finishing, finisher

fir   firs

fire   fires, fired, firing, fiery, fireplace, fireproof, fireworks, firewood

firm   firmer, firmest, firmly, firms, firmness, firming, firmed

first   firsthand

fish   fishing, fishes, fished, fishers, fisherman, fishermen, fishy

fit   fits, fitted, fitting

five   fifth, fifths, fifteen, fifteens, fifteenth, fifty, fifties, fiftieth

fix   fixes, fixed, fixing, fixer

flag   flags, flagging, flagged

flame   flames, flamed, flaming, flammable

flash   flashes, flashed, flashing, flashy, flashier, flasher, flashback

flashlight   flashlights

flat   flatter, flattest, flatly, flatten, flatness, flattening, flattener

flavor   flavors, flavored, flavoring, flavorful, flavorfully

flee   fled, flees, fleeing

flesh   fleshes, fleshed, fleshing, fleshy

float   floats, floated, floating

flock   flocks, flocking, flocked

flood   floods, flooded, flooding

floor   floors, floored, flooring, floorboard

flour   floury, floured, flouring

flower   flowers, flowered, flowery, flowering, flowerpot

fly

fly flew, flies, flying, flown, flier, flight

fog foggy, foggier, foggiest, foghorn

fold folded, folding, folds, folder

follow follows, followed, following, follower

fond fonder, fondest, fondly, fondness

fondle fondles, fondled, fondling

food foods, foodstuff

fool foolish, foolishly, fools, fooled, fooling

foot feet, foothill, footlights, footprint, footstep

football footballs

for

forbid forbids, forbidden, forbade, forbidding

force forces, forced, forcing, forceful, forcefulness, forcefully, forceable

ford fords, forded, fording, fordable

forehead foreheads

foreign foreigner, foreigners

forenoon forenoons

forest forests, forested, foresting, forestry, forester

forever

forfeit forfeits, forfeited, forfeiting

forget forgets, forgetting, forgotten, forgot, forgetfulness, forgetful, forgetfully, forgettable

forgive forgives, forgiving, forgave, forgiven, forgivable, forgiveness

fork forks, forked, forking

form forms, formed, forming

formal   formally, formality

former   formerly

fort   forts, fortify, fortified, fortifying

fortune   fortunes, fortunate, fortunately

forward   forwarded, forwarding

foul   fouls, fouled, fouling, fouler, foulest

found   founded, founding, foundation, foundations, foundational, founder

four   forty, fortieth, forties, fourteen

fowl   fowls

fox   foxes, foxlike, foxy

fracture   fractures, fractured, fracturing

fragrant   fragrantly, fragrance

frail   frailness, frailty

frame   frames, framed, framing, framer

frank   frankly, frankness

freckle   freckles, freckled, freckling, freckly

free   frees, freeing, freed, freedom, freedoms, freely, freer, freest

freeze   freezes, freezing, freezer, froze, frozen

freight   freights, freighted, freighting, freighter

fresh   fresher, freshest, freshly, freshen, freshness, freshman

Friday   Fri.

friend   friends, friendship, friendly, friendless, friendlier, friendliest

fright

fright frighten, frightened, frightening, frighteningly, frightful, frightfully

frog frogs, froglike

from

front fronts, frontier, frontiers, frontage

frost frosts, frosted, frosting, frosty

fruit fruits, fruity, fruitless, fruitful

fry fries, fried, frying, fryer

full fully, fullness, fill, filled, fuller, fullest

fun funny, funnier, funniest

funeral funerals

fur furs, furred, furrier, furry

furious furiously, fury, furiousness

furnace furnaces

furnish furnishes, furnished, furnishing, furniture

further furthered, furthering

future futures, futureless

gain gains, gained, gaining, gainful

gallery galleries

gallon gallons

gallop gallops, galloped, galloping

game games, gamely, gamy

gang gangs, ganged, ganging

garage garages, garaged

garbage

garden   gardens, gardened,
  gardening, gardener

gas   gases, gasoline, gassed

gate   gates, gateway

gather   gathers, gathered, gathering,
  gatherer

gay   gayer, gayest, gaily, gaiety

gear   gears, geared, gearing, gearless

general   generals, generally,
  generalize, generalizing, generalized

generate   generation, generations,
  generating, generated

gentle   gently, gentler, gentlest,
  gentleness

gentleman   gentlemen, gentlemanly

gentlewoman   gentlewomen

geography   geographies,
  geographical, geographically,
  geographer

germ   germs, germinate

get   gets, getting, got, gotten

ghost   ghosts, ghostly, ghostwriter,
  ghostlike

giant   gigantic, gigantically, giants,
  giantism, giantness

gift   gifts, gifted

giraffe   giraffes

girl   girls, girlish, girlhood

give   given, giving, giver, gave, gives

glad   gladness, gladder, gladdest,
  gladly, gladden, gladdened

glance   glances, glanced, glancing

glass

glass   glassful, glassware, glasses, glassy

glimpse   glimpsed, glimpsing, glimpses

globe   globes, global

gloom   gloomy, gloomier, gloomiest, gloomily, gloominess

glory   glorious, gloriously, gloriousness, glories, glorify

glove   gloves, gloved

glow   glows, glowed, glowing

go   goes, going, gone

goal   goals, goalie, goalkeeper

goat   goats, goatlike

gods   goddesses, godliness, godlike

gold   golden, gilt, gilded

golf   golfs, golfing, golfer

good   better, best, goods, goodly, goody, goodies, goodness

goose   geese

gopher   gophers

gorgeous   gorgeously, gorgeousness

gossip   gossips, gossiped, gossiping, gossiper, gossipy

govern   governs, governed, governing, government, governor, governors, governable, governess

gown   gowns, gowned

grab   grabs, grabbed, grabbing, grabby, grabber

grace   graceful, gracefully, gracefulness, gracious, graciously, graceless

grade   grades, graded, grading

gradual   gradually

graduate   graduated, graduating, graduation

grain   grains, grained, grainy, granular

grand   grander, grandest, grandly, grandeur

grandfather   grandfathers, grandpa

grandmother   grandmothers, grandma

grape   grapes, grapefruit

grass   grasses, grassed, grassy, grassing, grassier, grassiest

grateful   gratefully, gratefulness, gratitude

gravel   gravels, graveled, graveling, gravelly

gravy   gravies

gray   grays, grayed, graying, grayer, grayest, grayish, grayness

graze   grazes, grazing, grazed

grease   greases, greased, greasing, greasy, greasier, greasiest, greasiness

great   greater, greatest, greatly, greatness

green   greens, greenery, greener, greenest, greenish, greenness

greet   greets, greeted, greeting, greeter

grey   gray

grieve   grief, grieves, grieved, grieving

grind   grinds, grinding, grinder, ground, grounds

grocery   groceries, grocer

groove   grooves, grooved, grooving

ground   grounds, grounded, grounding

group   groups, grouped, grouping

grove   groves

grow   grows, grew, growing, growth, grown

growl   growls, growled, growling, growler

guard   guards, guarded, guarding, guardian

guess   guesses, guessing, guessed, guesser

guest   guests

guide   guides, guided, guiding, guidance, guidelines

gulf   gulfs

gum   gums, gummed, gumming, gummy

gun   guns, gunfight, gunfire

guy   guys

gym   gyms, gymnasium, gymnastic, gymnast

habit   habits, habitual, habitually

had   has, have, had, having, hasn't, haven't, hadn't

hadn't   had not

hail   hails, hailed, hailing

hair   hairs, hairy, hairless, hairiest

half   halves, halfback, halfway

hall   halls, hallway

Halloween

ham   hams, hammy

hammer   hammers, hammered, hammering

hand   hands, handing, handed, handful, handfuls

handkerchief   handkerchiefs

handle   handles, handled, handling

handsome   handsomer, handsomest, handsomely

handy   handier, handiest, handily, handiness

hang   hangs, hanging, hanger, hanged, hung, hangman

happen   happens, happened, happening, happenings

happy   happier, happiest, happily, happiness

harbor   harbors, harbored, harboring

hard   harder, hardest, hardly, hardness, hardens, hardened, hardening, hardener

hardware

harm   harms, harmed, harming, harmful, harmless, harmfully, harmlessly

harvest   harvests, harvested, harvesting, harvester

has   have, had, having, hadn't, haven't, hasn't

haste   hasten, hastens, hastened, hastening, hastily, hasty, hastiness, hastier, hastiest

hat   hats, hatter

hatch

hatch hatches, hatched, hatching, hatcher, hatchery

hatchet hatchets

hate hates, hated, hating, hateful, hatefully, hatefulness

haul hauls, hauled, hauling, hauler

haunt haunted, haunts

have has, had, having, haven't, hasn't, hadn't

hawk hawks, hawkish

hay hays, hayed, haying, hayloft, haystack, hayseed

he him, his, he'd, he's, he'll

head heads, header, headed, heading, heady

headache headaches

headquarters headquartering

health healthy, healthier, healthiest, healthful

heap heaps, heaped, heaping

hear hears, hearing, heard

heart hearts, heartache, heartbeat

heat heats, heated, heating, heater

heaven heavens, heavenly, heavenward

heavy heavier, heaviest, heavily, heaviness

heel heels, heeled, heeling

height heights, heightened

held hold

helicopter helicopters

hello hellos, helloed

helmet helmets, helmeted

help helps, helper, helping, helped, helpful, helpfully, helpfulness, helpless, helplessly, helplessness

hen hens, henhouse

her hers, herself, she

herd herds, herded, herding

here hereby, hereafter, herein

hero heroes, heroic, heroically, heroism

hesitate hesitates, hesitated, hesitating, hesitatingly, hesitation

hi hello

hide hid, hides, hidden, hiding, hideaway

high higher, highest, highly, highness, height, heightened

highway highways

hike hikes, hiked, hiker, hiking

hill hills, hilly, hillside

him himself, he, his

hind hinds, hindsight

hinge hinges, hinged, hinging

history histories, historian, historic, historical, historically

hit hits, hitter, hitting

hitch hitches, hitched, hitching

hobby hobbies

hockey

hog hogs, hogged, hogging

hold holds, holder, holding, held

hole holes, holed, holey

holiday holidays

hollow

hollow   hollows, hollowed, hollowing

holly   hollies

holy   holier, holiest

home   homes, homing, homeward

homesick   homesickness

homework

honest   honesty, honestly

honey   honeys, honied

honor   honors, honored, honoring, honorable, honorably

hood   hoods, hooded

hook   hooks, hooked, hooking, hooklike

hop   hops, hopped, hopper, hopping

hope   hopes, hoped, hoping, hopeful, hopefully, hopeless, hopelessly

horizon   horizons, horizontal, horizontally

horn   horns, horny, horned, hornless

horrid   horridly, horridness

horror   horrors, horrible, horribly, horrify, horrifies, horrified, horrifying

horse   horses, horseback, horseless, horsy

hose   hoses, hosed, hosing

hospital   hospitals, hospitalizing, hospitalized

hot   hotter, hottest, hotly, hotness, heat, heated, heats, heating

hotel   hotels

hour   hours, hourly

house   houses, housing, housed, household

how

however

howl   howls, howled, howling, howler

hug   hugs, hugged, hugging

huge   hugeness

hull   hulls, hulled, hulling

human   humanly, humans, humanity,
humane, humanely

humor   humors, humored, humoring,
humorist, humorous, humorously

hundred   hundreds, hundredth

hunger   hungered, hungering,
hungers, hungry

hunt   hunter, hunting, hunted,
huntsman, hunts

hurry   hurries, hurried, hurrying

hurt   hurts, hurting, hurtful

husband   husbands

hut   huts

hygiene   hygienic, hygienically,
hygienist

hymn   hymns, hymnal

I   I'm, I'll, I've, I'd

ice   iced, icing, ices, icy, iceberg

ice cream   ice creams

icicle   icicles

idea   ideas

ideal   ideally, idealism, idealistic

idle

idle idly, idleness, idled, idling

if

ignore ignores, ignored, ignoring, ignorance, ignorant, ignorantly, ignoramus

ill ills, illness

imagine imagines, imagined, imagining, imagination, imaginative, imaginatively

immense immensely, immensity

import imports, importer, imported, importing

important importantly, importance

impossible impossibly, impossibility

impress impression, impressions, impressionable, impressive

improve improves, improved, improving, improvement

improvise improvisation

in into, inner, innermost, inward

inch inches, inched, inching

incident incidents, incidental, incidentally

include includes, included, including, inclusive, inclusively

income incomes

incorrect incorrectly, incorrectness

increase increases, increased, increasing, increasingly

indeed

independent independently, independence

Indian Indians

indicate   indicates, indicated, indicating, indication, indicator

individual   individuals, individually, individualist, individualistic, individuality, individualize

industry   industries, industrial, industrious, industrialize, industriously

infant   infants, infancy, infantile

influence   influences, influencing, influential

inform   informs, informed, informer, informing, information

initial   initials, initialed, initialing, initially

injure   injured, injuring, injures, injury, injuries, injurious

inning   innings

innocent   innocently, innocence

inquire   inquires, inquirer, inquired, inquiring, inquiringly, inquiry

insect   insects, insecticide

inside   insides, insider

insist   insists, insisted, insisting, insistence, insistent, insistently

inspect   inspects, inspected, inspector, inspecting, inspection

instance   instant, instants, instantly, instantaneous, instantaneously

instead

instruct   instructs, instructed, instructor, instructing, instruction

instrument   instruments, instrumental, instrumentally, instrumentalist, instrumentation

insure

insure insures, insured, insuring, insurance

intellect intellectual, intellectually

intelligent intelligently, intelligence

intend intends, intended, intending, intention, intentional, intentionally, intent

interest interests, interested, interesting, interestingly

interfere interferes, interfered, interfering, interference

interior interiors, internal

interrupt interrupts, interrupted, interrupting, interruption

interval intervals

interview interviews, interviewer, interviewing, interviewed

into

introduce introduces, introduced, introducing, introduction

invent invents, invented, inventor, inventing, invention, inventive

invest invests, invested, investor, investing, investment

invisible invisibility, invisibly

invite invites, invited, inviting, invitation

iron irons, ironed, ironing

irony ironic

irrigate irrigates, irrigated, irrigating, irrigation

is isn't

island islands, islander

issue issues, issued, issuing

it   its, it's

itself

jacket   jackets, jacketed

jail   jails, jailed, jailing, jailer

January   Jan.

jar   jars, jarred, jarring, jarful

jealous   jealously, jealousy

jelly   jellies, jellied, jellying, jell

jerk   jerks, jerked, jerking, jerky, jerkiest, jerkily

jet   jets, jetted, jetting

jewel   jewels, jewelry

job   jobs

join   joins, joiner, joined, joining

joint   joints, jointed, jointly

joke   jokes, joked, joking, jokingly, joker

journal   journalism

journey   journeys, journeyed, journeying

joy   joyful, joyous, joyless, joyfulness, joyfully, joyously

judge   judges, judged, judging, judgment

juice   juicy, juices, juiciness, juicier, juiciest

July

jump   jumps, jumped, jumping, jumper, jumpy

June

June

jungle   jungles

junior   Jr.

jury   juries, juror

just   justly, justify, justified, justifying, justification, justice

keep   keeps, keeper, keeping, kept

kettle   kettles

key   keys, keyboard

kick   kicks, kicked, kicker, kicking

kid   kids, kidding, kidded, kiddingly

kill   killed, killing, kills, killer

kind   kinds, kinder, kindest, kindly, kindness

kindergarten   kindergartens, kindergartener

kindle   kindles, kindled, kindling

king   kings, kingly, kingdom, kingdoms

kiss   kisses, kissed, kissing, kisser

kitchen   kitchens

kite   kites, kiting

kitten   kittens, kitty, cat

knee   kneel, knees, kneels, kneeled, knelt, kneeler, kneeling, kneecap

knife   knives, knifed, knifing

knight   knights, knighted, knighthood

knit   knits, knitted

knock   knocks, knocker, knocked, knocking

knot   knots, knotted, knotting, knotty

know   knew, knows, knowing, knowingly, known, knowledge

labor   labors, laborer, labored, laboring

laboratory   laboratories

lace   laces, laced, lacing, lacy

lack   lacks, lacked, lacking, lackadaisical

lad   lads, laddy

ladder   ladders

lady   ladies, ladylike

lake   lakes, lakeside, lakeshore

lamp   lamps

land   lands, landed, landing, landlord, landlady

language   languages

lantern   lanterns

large   largest, largely, enlarge, enlargement

last   lasts, lasted, lastingly, lastly, lastingly

late   later, latest, lately, lateness

latter

laugh   laughs, laughed, laughing, laughingly, laughable

launch   launches, launched, launching

laundry

laundry laundries, launder, laundromat, laundered, laundering

law lawyer, lawyers, laws, lawless

lawn lawns

lay laid, lays, laying, lain, layer

lazy lazier, laziest, lazily, laziness

lead leads, leader, leading, leaderless, led

leaf leafed, leafing, leaves, leafage, leafless, leafy, leaflet

league leagues

leak leaks, leaked, leaking, leaky

lean leans, leaner, leanest, leaned, leaning

leap leaped, leapt, leaps, leaping, leapfrog

learn learns, learner, learned, learning

leather leathers, leathery

leave leaves, leaving, left

leg legs, leggy, legged

legal legally, legality, legalize, legalizing, legalized

legislate legislator, legislature, legislation, legislative

leisure leisurely

lemon lemons, lemony, lemonade

lend lent, lending, lends, lender

length lengths, lengthy, lengthened, lengthening

less lesser, lessen, lessened, lessening, least

lesson lessons

let lets, letting, let's

letter letters, lettering, lettered

lettuce lettuces

levee levees

level levels, leveled, leveling

levy levies, levied, levying

liberty liberties, liberate, liberator, liberated, liberating, liberation

library libraries, librarian

license licenses, licensed, licensing

lie lies, lying, liar, lied, lay, lain

lieutenant lieutenants

life lives, live, lived, living, lively, livelier, lifeboat, lifeguard, lifesaver

lift lifts, lifted, lifting

light lighter, lightest, lightly, lighting, lightness, lights, lighten, lighter

lightning

like likes, liked, likely, liking, likeness, likenesses, likelier, likeliest, liken

limit limits, limited, limiting, limitation, limitless

limp limper, limpest, limply, limps, limped, limping

line lines, liner, lining, linear, lineman

linen linens

lion lions, lioness, lionhearted

liquid liquids, liquify, liquified, liquifies

liquidate liquidation

listen listens, listener, listened, listening

literature literary, literate, literacy

little

little littler, littlest, littleness

load loads, loader, loaded, loading

loaf loafs, loafer, loafing, loaves

loan loans, loaned, loaning, lend

local locally, locality, localize

locate locates, located, locating, location

lock locked, locking, locks, locker, locket

lodge lodges, lodger, lodged, lodging

log logs, logger, logged, logging

lone lonely, lonesome, lonelier, loneliest, loneliness

long longer, longest, longs, longing, longed, longish, length

look looks, looked, looking, lookout

loop loops, looped, looping

loose looser, loosest, loosen, loosens, loosened, loosening, loosely

lose loses, lost, losing, loser, loss, losses

lot lots

loud louder, loudest, loudness, loudmouth, loudly

love loves, lover, loved, loving, lovable

lovely lovelier, loveliest, loveliness

low lower, lowest, lowered, lowering, lowly

loyal loyally, loyalty, loyalist

luck lucky, luckier, luckiest, luckily

lump lumps, lumped, lumping, lumpy, lumpiness

lunch luncheon, luncheons

lung lungs

luster lusters, lustrous, lustrously

luxury luxuries, luxurious, luxuriously

machine machines, machinery, machinist, mechanical

mad madder, maddest, madden, maddening, maddened

magazine magazines

magic magical, magically, magician

magnificent magnificently, magnificence

maid maids, maiden

mail mails, mailed, mailing, mailman, mailbox, mailbag

major majors, majority

make makes, maker, making, made

mammal mammals

man manned, manning, manly, mannish, men, mankind

manage manages, manager, managed, managing, manageable, management

mane manes

manner manners, mannered, mannerly, mannerism

manual manually

manufacture manufactures, manufacturer, manufactured, manufacturing

many

map

map   maps, mapped, mapping

maple   maple syrup

March   Mar.

march   marches, marcher, marched, marching

margin   margins, margined, marginal

mark   marks, marked, marking

market   markets, marketing, marketed

marry   marries, married, marrying, marriage

marvel   marvels, marveled, marveling, marvelous, marvelously

mass   masses, massed, massing, massive

master   masters, mastered, mastering, mastery

match   matched, matching, matches, matchbook, matchbox, matchless

material   materials, materialism

mathematics   mathematical, mathematician

matter   matters, mattered

May

maybe   may

mayor   mayors, mayoress

me   mine, my

meadow   meadows

meal   meals, mealy, mealtime

mean   means, meant, meaning, meaner, meanest, meaningful, meanness, meanly

meantime

meanwhile

measure   measures, measured, measuring, measurement

meat   meats, meaty, meatball, meatless

mechanic   mechanics, mechanism, mechanize, mechanical, mechanically

medal   medals, medallion

medicine   medicines, medical, medically, medicate, medication, medic

medium   mediums, media, median, medial

meet   meets, meeting, met

melt   melts, melted, melting, molten

member   members, membership

memorial

memory   memories, memorize, memorizes, memorized, memorizing, memorization

mend   mends, mended, mending

mention   mentions, mentioned, mentioning

merchant   merchants

mere   merely

merry   merrier, merriest, merrily, merriment

mess   messing, messes, messy

message   messages, messenger

metal   metals, metallic

meter   meters, metered, metric, m.

method   methods, methodical, methodically

middle

middle midst

midnight midnights

might mighty, mightier, mightiest, mightily

mild milder, mildest, mildly, mildness

mile miles, miler, mileage

milk milked, milking, milky

mill mills, milling, milled, miller

million millions, millionth

mind minds, minded, minding, mindful

mine mines, mined, mining, miner, minefield

mineral minerals, minerology, minerologist

minister ministers, ministry

minor minors

minority minorities

mint mints, minty, minted, minting

minute minutes, minutely, minuteman

mischief mischievous, mischievously

miserable miserably, misery, miseries

miss misses, missed, missing

misspell misspells, misspelled, misspelling

mist mists, misty

mistake mistaking, mistakes, mistaken, mistakenly

misuse misuses, misused, misusing, misusage

mix mixes, mixed, mixing, mixer, mixture

modern modernistic

moist moisten, moistens, moistened, moistening, moisture, moistness

mom mommy, mama, mother, momma

moment moments, momentary, momentarily

Monday Mon.

money monies, moneys, moneyed, moneybag

monkey monkeys, monkeyed, monkeying

monster monsters, monstrous, monstrosity

month months, monthly

monument monuments, monumental, monumentally

mood moods, moody, moodily, moodiness

moon moons, moonbeam, moonlight

moose

more moreover

morning mornings

mosquito mosquitoes, mosquitoey

moss mossy, mosses, mosslike

most mostly

mother mothers, motherhood, motherly

mothered mothering

motion motions, motioned, motioning, motionless, motionlessly

motor motors, motored, motoring, motorboat, motorbike, motorist, motorize

motto

motto   mottos

mountain   mountains, mountaineer, mountainside, mountainous

mouse   mice, mousetrap, mousy

mouth   mouths, mouthful

move   moves, mover, moved, moving, movable

movie   movies

mow   mowed, mown, mowing, mows

Mr.   mister

Mrs.   mistress

Ms.

much

mud   muddy, muddier, muddiest, muddies, muddied, muddying

multiply   multiplies, multiplied, multiplying, multiple, multiplication, multiplier, multiplicand

murder   murders, murdered, murdering, murderer, murderous

muscle   muscles, muscled, muscling, muscular

museum   museums

music   musician, musicians, musical, musically

must

my   myself

mystery   mysteries, mysterious, mysteriously

nail   nails, nailed, nailing

name   names, named, naming, namely, nameless, namesake

narrow   narrower, narrowest, narrowly

nation   nations, national, nationally, nationality

nature   natures, natural, naturally, naturalize

naughty   naughtier, naughtiest

navy   navies, naval

near   nears, neared, nearing, nearer, nearest, nearly

neat   neater, neatest, neatness, neatly

necessary   necessarily, necessity, necessities

neck   necks, necklace, neckline

necktie   neckties

need   needs, needed, needing, needy, needless, needlessly, neediness

needle   needles, needled, needling, needlework

neglect   neglects, neglected, neglecting, neglectful, negligence, negligent

Negro   Negroes, Negroid

neighbor   neighbors, neighboring, neighborly, neighborhood, neighborhoods

neither   nor

nephew   nephews

nerve   nerves, nervy, nervous, nervously, nervousness

nest   nests, nested, nesting

net   nets, netted, netting

never

never nevermore, nevertheless

new news, newer, newest, newness, newly

news newspaper, newspapers, newscast, newscaster, newsprint, newsboy

next

nice nicer, nicest, niceness, nicely

nickel nickels

niece nieces

night nights, nightfall, nightgown, nighttime, nighty, nightmare

nine nines, ninth, nineteen, nineteens, nineteenth, ninety, nineties, ninetieth

no none, not, nothing

noble nobles, nobler, noblest, nobility

nobody

noise noises, noisier, noisiest, noisily

nonsense nonsensical

noodle noodles

noon noontime, noonday

nope

nor neither

normal normally, normality

north northern, northerly, northward

nose noses, nosed, nosing, nosy, nosier, nosiest

note notes, noted, noting, notable, notably, notation

nothing

notice notices, noticed, noticing, noticeable, noticeably

notify   notifies, notified, notifying, notification

November   Nov.

now

nowhere

nuisance   nuisances

number   numbers, numbered, numbering

numeral   numerals, numerous

nurse   nurses, nursed, nursing

nut   nuts, nutty, nuttiest

oak   oaks, oaken, oaklike

oat   oats, oatmeal

obey   obeys, obeyed, obeying, obedient, obediently, obedience

object   objects, objected, objecting, objection

obtain   obtains, obtained, obtaining, obtainable

occasion   occasions, occasional, occasionally, occasioned

occupation   occupations, occupational

occupy   occupies, occupied, occupying, occupant, occupancy

occur   occurs, occurred, occurring, occurrence

ocean   oceanography, oceanic

o'clock

October   Oct.

odd

odd odder, oddest, oddness, oddity

of

off

offend offends, offended, offending, offender

offense offenses, offensive, offensively

offer offers, offered, offering

office offices, officer, official, officially, officiate

often oftener, oftenest

oh

oil oils, oiled, oiling, oily

okay ok

old older, olden, oldest

omit omits, omitted, omitting, omission

on onto

once

one ones

one half halves

onion

only

open opens, opened, opening, opener, openly

opera operas, operetta, operatic

operate operates, operator, operated, operating, operation

opinion opinions, opinionated

oppose opposes, opposed, opposing, opposite, opposition

or nor

orange   oranges, orangeade

orbit   orbits, orbited, orbiting, orbital

orchard   orchards

order   orders, ordered, ordering, orderly

ordinary   ordinarily

ore   ores

organ   organs, organist

organic   organism

organize   organizes, organized, organizing, organization, organizational, organizer

original   originals, originally, originality, originate, originator, origin

other   others

otherwise

ought

our   ours, ourselves

out   outer, outing, outward, outermost, outbreak, outcome

outdoors   outdoor

outfit   outfits, outfitted, outfitter, outfitting

outline   outlines, outlined, outlining

outside   outsides, outsider

outstanding

oven   ovens

over

overcome   overcomes, overcame, overcoming

overflow   overflows, overflowed, overflowing

overturn   overturns, overturned, overturning

owe   owes, owed, owing

owl   owls, owlish

own   owns, owner, owned, owning, ownership

oyster   oysters

pace   paced, pacing, paces, pacemaker

pack   packs, packer, packing, package

page   pages, paged, paging

pageant   pageants, pageantry

pain   pains, pained, paining, painful, painfully

paint   paints, painter, painted, painting

pair   pairs, paired, pairing

pajamas

palace   palaces, palatial

pale   paler, palest, paled, paling

palm   palms, palmed, palming, palmist

pan   pans, panning, panned

pancake

pants

papa   papas

paper   papers, papered, papering, paperweight

parade   parading, parades, paraded

paragraph paragraphs, paragraphed, paragraphing

parallel parallels, paralleled, paralleling

parcel parcels, parcelled, parcelling

park parks, parked, parking

part parts, parted, parting, partly, partner

particular particulars, particularly

partner partners, partnership

party parties, partied, partying

pass passes, passed, passing, passer, passable, past

passage passenger

paste pastes, pasted, pasting

pasture pastures, pastured, pasturing

patch patches, patched, patching

patent patents

path paths, pathway

patient patiently, patience

patrol patrols, patrolled, patrolling, patrolman

pattern patterns, patterned, patterning

pause pauses, paused, pausing

pave paves, paved, paving, pavement, pavements

pay pays, paid, paying, payment, payable

pea peas, peapod

peace peaceful, peacefully

peanut peanuts

pecan   pecans

peculiar   peculiarly, peculiarity, peculiarities

pen   pens

pencil   pencils

penny   pennies, penniless

people   peoples, peopled, peopling

per

percent   percentage, percentages, percentile

perform   performs, performed, performer, performing, performance

perfume   perfumes, perfumer, perfumed

perhaps

period   periods, periodical, periodically

permanent   permanently, permanence

permit   permits, permitted, permitting, permission, permissible, permissive

person   persons, personal, personally, personality, personable

persuade   persuades, persuaded, persuading, persuasion, persuasive, persuasively

pet   pets, petted, petting

phone   phones, phoned, phoning

photograph   photographs, photography, photographed, photographing, photographic

phrase   phrases, phrased, phrasing

physical   physically, physique

physician   physicians

piano   pianos

pick   picks, picker, pickers, picked, picking

pickle   pickles, pickled, pickling

picnic   picnics, picnicked, picnicking, picnicker

picture   pictures, pictured, picturing, picturesque

pie   pies

piece   pieces, piecemeal

pier   piers

pierce   pierces, piercing, pierced, piercingly

pig   pigs, piglet, pigpen

pigeon   pigeons

pile   piles, piled, piling

pilgrim   pilgrims, pilgrimage

pillow   pillows

pin   pins, pinned, pinning

pine   pines, pinelike

pineapple   pineapples

pink   pinks, pinker, pinkest, pinky

pint   pints

pipe   pipes, piped, piping, pipeline

pirate   pirates, pirated, pirating

pistol   pistols

pit   pits, pitted, pitting

pitch   pitches, pitcher, pitched, pitching

pity   pities, pitied, pitying, pitiful, pitifully

place

place places, placed, placing, placement

plain plainer, plainest, plainly, plainness

plan plans, planner, planned, planning

plane planes, planed, planing

planet planets, planetarium, planetary

plank planks

plant plants, planter, planted, planting

plantation plantations

plaster plasters, plasterer, plastered, plastering

plastic plastics

plate plates, plated, plating

plateau plateaus

platform platforms

play plays, player, played, playing, playful, playfully

playground playgrounds

playmate playmates

please pleases, pleaser, pleased, pleasing, pleasant, pleasantly

pleasure pleasures, pleasurable, pleasurably

pledge pledges, pledged, pledging

plenty plentiful, plentifully

P.M.

pocket pockets, pocketed, pocketing

poem poems, poet, poetry

point points, pointer, pointed, pointing, pointedly

poison   poisons, poisoned, poisoning

poke   pokes, poker, poked, poking

pole   poles, poled, poling

police   policeman, policemen, policewomen

policy   policies

polish   polishes, polisher, polished, polishing

polite   politeness

politic   politics, political, politically, politician

pollute   pollution, polluted, polluting, pollutes, pollutant

pond   ponds, pondlike

pony   ponies

pool   pools, pooled, pooling, poolroom

poor   poorer, poorest, poorly, poverty

pop   pops, popped, popping

popcorn

popular   popularly, popularity

porch   porches

pork   porker

porridge   porringer

porter   porters, portage

portion   portioned, portioning

position   positions, positioned, positioning

positive   positively

possess   possessor, possesses, possessed, possessing, possession

possible   possibly, possibilities

post

post   postal, postage, posts, posted, posting

poster   posters

postman   postmen

postmaster   postmasters, postmistress

post office   post offices

postpone   postpones, postponed, postponing, postponement

potato   potatoes

poultry

pound   pounds, pounded, pounding

pour   pours, poured, pouring

powder   powders, powdered, powdering

power   powers, powered, powering, powerful, powerfully

practical   practically

practice   practices, practiced, practicing, practitioner

prairie   prairies

praise   praises, praised, praising

pray   prays, prayer, prayed, praying

preach   preaches, preacher, preached, preaching

precious   preciously

prefer   prefers, preferred, preferring, preference, preferable, preferably

prepare   prepares, prepared, preparing, preparation, preparedly, preparatory

present   presents, presented, presenting, presence, presentable, presentation

preside   presides, presided,
  presiding, president, presidential

press   presses, pressed, pressing

pressure   pressures, pressured,
  pressuring

pretend   pretends, pretended,
  pretending, pretense

pretty   prettily, prettier, prettiest,
  prettiness

prevail   prevails, prevailed, prevailing,
  prevalent

prevent   prevents, prevented,
  preventing, prevention

previous   previously

price   prices, priced, pricing

pride   proud, proudly

priest   priests, priestly

prim   primmer, primmest

prime   primary, primaries, primarily,
  primate

prince   princes, princely, princess

principal   principals

principle   principles, principled

print   prints, printed, printer, printing

prison   prisons, prisoner, imprisoned,
  imprisoning

private   privately, privacy

privilege   privileges, privileged,
  privileging

prize   prizes, prized, prizing

probable   probably, probability

problem   problems

procedure   procedures

proceed

proceed proceeds, proceeded, proceeding, procession, processional

process processes, processed, processing

produce produces, producer, produced, producing, production

product products, production, productive

profess professor, professors

profit profits, profitted, profitting, profitable

program programed, programs, programing

progress progresses, progressed, progressing, progressive

prominent prominently, prominence

promise promises, promised, promising

prompt prompter, promptly, promptness

pronounce pronounces, pronounced, pronouncing, pronunciation

proof proofs, prove, proves, proved, proving, proven

proper properly

propose proposes, proposed, proposing, proposal, proposition

prosper prospers, prospered, prospering, prosperous, prosperity

protect protects, protected, protector, protecting, protection, protective

protest protests, protested, protesting

proud   prouder, proudest, proudly, pride

provide   provides, provider, provided, providing, provision

prune   prunes, pruned, pruning

public   publically, publicity

publish   publishes, publisher, published, publishing, publication

puck   pucks, pucker

pull   pulls, puller, pulled, pulling

pump   pumps, pumper, pumped, pumping

pumpkin   pumpkins

punch   punches, punched, punching, punchy

punctual   punctually, punctuality

punish   punishes, punished, punishing, punishment, punishable

pup   pups, puppy, puppies, puppyish

pupil   pupils

puppet   puppets, puppeteer

purchase   purchases, purchaser, purchased, purchasing

pure   purely, purer, purest, purity, purify, purifies, purified, purifying, pureness

purple   purples, purplish

purpose   purposeful, purposeless

purse   purses, pursed, pursing

pursue   pursues, pursuer, pursued, pursuing, pursuit

push   pushes, pusher, pushed, pushing, pushy

put

put   puts, putting

putt   putts, putting, putted, putter

puzzle   puzzles, puzzled, puzzler, puzzling

quality   qualities

qualify   qualifies, qualified, qualifying

quantity   quantities

quart   quarts

quarter   quarters, quartered, quartering, quarterly

queen   queens, queenly

queer   queerer, queerest, queerly, queerness

question   questions, questioned, questioner, questioning, questioningly, questionnaire

quick   quicker, quickest, quickly

quiet   quieter, quietest, quietly, quietness

quit   quitter, quitting, quits

quite

quote   quotes, quoted, quoting, quotation

rabbit   rabbits

race   races, racer, raced, racing

racket   rackets, racquet

radiate   radiates, radiated, radiators, radiating, radiation

radio   radios, radioed

radish   radishes

rag   rags, ragged, raggedly, raggedness

raid   raids, raided, raider, raiding

rail   rails, railway, railroad, railroads

rain   rains, rainy, rained, raining, rainiest, rainbow, rainshower, raincoat

raise   raises, raised, raising

raisin   raisins

rake   rakes, raked, raking

rally   rallies, rallied, rallying

ranch   ranches, rancher, ranching

rang   ring

range   ranges, ranger, ranged, ranging

rank   ranks, ranked, ranking

rapid   rapidly, rapidness

rare   rarely, rarer, rarest, rarity

rascal   rascals, rascally

rat   rats, ratty, ratlike

rate   rates, rated, rating

rather

ray   rays, rayed, raying

reach   reaches, reached, reaching

read   reader, reads, reading

ready   readier, readiest, readily, readies, readying, readied, readiness

real   really, realize, reality

realize

realize   realizes, realization, realized, realizing

reason   reasons, reasoned, reasoning

receive   receipt, receipts, receives, received, receiving, receiver, reception

recent   recently, recentness

recess   recesses, recessed, recessing

reckless   recklessly, recklessness

recognize   recognizes, recognizing, recognizable, recognition

recommend   recommends, recommended, recommending, recommendation

record   records, recorded, recording, recorder

recover   recovers, recovered, recovery, recovering

red   redder, reddest, redness, redwood, redhead, reddish, redden, redcoat

reduce   reduces, reduced, reducing, reduction

refer   refers, referred, referral, referring, referable, reference

reform   reforms, reformed, reformer, reforming

refrigerate   refrigerated, refrigerates, refrigerating

refrigerator   refrigerators

refuse   refuses, refused, refusal, refusing

regain   regains, regained, regaining

regard   regards, regarded, regarding, regardless

region   regions, regional

register   registers, registered, registrar, registering, registration, registry

regret   regrets, regretted, regretting, regettable, regretful

regular   regularly, regularity, regulate, regulation

reign   reigns, reigned, reigning, rule

reindeer

relative   relatives, relatively, relation, relativity

release   releases, released, releasing

relief   reliefs, relieve, relieves, relieved, relieving

religion

religious   religiously

remain   remains, remained, remainder, remaining

remark   remarks, remarkable, remarkably, remarking, remarked

remedy   remedies, remedied

remember   remembered, remembrance, remembering, remembers

remind   reminds, reminded, reminder, reminding, remember

remove   removes, removed, remover, removing, removable

render   rendered, rendering, renders

rent   rents, rented, renting, rental

repair   repairs, repaired, repairing, repairman

repeat   repeated, repeating, repeats

reply   replies, replied, replying

report

report   reports, reporter, reported, reporting

represent   represents, represented, representing, representative, representation

republic   republics, republican

request   requests, requested, requesting, requisition

require   requires, required, requiring, requirement

resemble   resembles, resembled, resembling, resemblance

reserve   reserves, reserved, reserving, reservation, reservoir

reside   resides, resided, residing, resident, residence, residential

resist   resistant, resistance

resort   resorts

respect   respects, respected, respecting, respectful, respectfully, respectable

respond   responds, responded, responding, response

rest   rests, rested, resting, restless, restlessness, restful

restaurant   restaurants, restauranteur

result   results, resulted, resulting

retreat   retreats, retreated, retreating

return   returns, returned, returning, returnable

reverse   reverses, reversed, reversing, reversal, reversible

revolt   revolted, revolting, revolution, revolutionary

reward   rewards, rewarded, rewarding

ribbon   ribbons

rice   rices, riced, ricing

rich   richer, richest, richly

ride   riding, rides, rode, ridden, rider

right   rights, righted, righting

ring   ringing, rings, rung, ringer

rip   ripped, rips, ripping, ripper

rise   rises, rising, risen, rose

risk   risked, risks, risking, risky

river   rivers, riverbed, riverside

road   roads, roadblock, roadside, roadway

roam   roams, roamed, roaming

roar   roars, roared, roaring, roarer

roast   roasts, roasted, roasting

robin   robins

robot   robots, robotism

rock   rocks, rocky, rockiest

rocket   rocketed, rocketing

rod   rods

roll   rolls, roller, rolled, rolling

roof   roofs, roofing, roofer

room   rooms, roomed, rooming, roommate, roomful, roomy

rooster   roosters

root   roots, rooted, rooting

rope   ropes, roped, roping

rose   roses, rosebush

rot   rots, rotten, rotted, rotting

rough   rougher, roughest, roughness

round

round   rounded, rounding, rounder, roundest

route   routes, routed, routing

row   rows, rower, rowed, rowing

rub   rubs, rubbed, rubbing

rubber   rubbers, rubbery

rude   ruder, rudest, rudeness, rudely

ruin   ruins, ruined, ruining

rule   rules, ruler, ruled, ruling, reign

run   running, ran, runs, runner

runaway   runaways

rush   rushes, rusher, rushed, rushing

sack   sacks, sacked, sacking

sacred   sacredly, sacredness

sad   sadly, sadder, sadden, saddest, saddened, saddening, sadness

saddle   saddles, saddled, saddling

safe   safes, safer, safely, safety, safest

sail   sails, sailed, sailing, sailor, sailors

sake   sakes

salad   salads

salary   salaries, salaried

sale   salesman, saleswoman, salesperson, salesclerk

salt   salts, salted, salting, salty

salute   salutes, saluted, saluting, salutation

same sameness

sand sands, sander, sanded, sanding, sandy, sandiest, sandpaper, sandpile, sandstorm

sanitary sanitarily, sanitation

satin satins, satiny

satisfy satisfies, satisfied, satisfying, satisfyingly, satisfactory, satisfactorily, satisfaction

Saturday Sat.

sauce sauces, sauced, saucing, saucy, saucier, sauciest

saucer saucers

sausage sausages

savage savages, savagely

save saves, saver, saved, saving, savings, savior

say says, saying, said

scale scales, scaler, scaled, scaling, scaly, scalier, scaliest

scar scars, scarred, scarring, scarifies, scarified, scarifying

scarce scarcer, scarcest, scarcely, scarceness, scarcity

scare scares, scaring, scared, scary, scarier, scariest

scarf scarves

scatter scatters, scattered, scattering

scene scenes, scenic, scenery

scent scents, scented, scenting

scheme schemes, schemed, scheming, schemer

scholar scholars, scholarly, scholastic, scholastically

school

school   schools, schooling, schooled

schoolmate   schoolmates

schoolroom   schoolrooms

science   sciences, scientific, scientist, scientists, scientifically

scissors   scissored, scissoring

scold   scolds, scolded, scolding

score   scores, scored, scoring, scorecard

scowl   scowls, scowled, scowling

scramble   scrambles, scrambled, scrambling

scrap   scraps, scrapped, scrapper, scrapping, scrappy

scratch   scratches, scratched, scratcher, scratching, scratchy

scream   screams, screamed, screaming, screamer

screen   screens, screened, screening

screw   screws, screwed, screwing

screwdriver   screwdrivers

scrub   scrubs, scrubber, scrubbed, scrubbing

sea   seas, seaward, seagoing, seaport, seashore, seaweed

seal   seals, sealer, sealed, sealing

search   searches, searcher, searched, searching

season   seasons, seasoned, seasoning

seat   seats, seated, seating

second   seconds, secondly, secondary

secret   secretly, secrecy

secretary   secretaries, secretarial

secure   secures, secured, securing, securely, security

see   seeing, saw, seen

seed   seeds, seeded, seeding, seedless, seedling, seedy

seek   sought, seeking, seeks

seem   seems, seemed, seeming

seize   seizes, seized, seizing, seizure

seldom

select   selects, selected, selecting, selection

self   selves

selfish   selfishly, selfishness

sell   sold, selling, sells, seller

senate   senator, senators, senatorial

send   sends, sender, sending, sent

senior   seniors, seniority

sensation   sensational, sensationally

sense   senses, sensed, sensing, sensory, sensual

sentence   sentences, sentenced, sentencing

sentiment   sentiments, sentimental, sentimentally, sentimentalist

separate   separates, separated, separator, separating, separation

September   Sept.

serious   seriously, seriousness

sermon   sermons

serve   serves, server, served, serving, service, servant, servants

session   sessions

set

set   sets, setting, setback, setup, setoff

settle   settles, settler, settled, settling, settlement

seven   sevens, seventeen, seventh, seventy, seventieth

several

severe   severely, severity

sew   sews, sewed, sewing, sewn

shack   shacks

shades   shaded, shading, shady

shadow   shadows, shadowed, shadowing, shadowy

shaft   shafts

shake   shakes, shaking, shook, shaky, shakily, shaker, shakier, shakiest

shame   shames, shamed, shaming, shameful, shameless

shape   shapes, shaped, shaping, shapely

share   shares, sharer, shared, sharing

sharp   sharper, sharpest, sharply, sharpness, sharpening, sharpened

she   she's, she'd

shed   sheds, shedder, shedding

sheep   shepherd, sheepfold, sheepish, sheepskin

sheet   sheets, sheeted, sheeting

shell   shells, shelled, shelling

shelter   shelters, sheltered, sheltering

sheriff   sheriffs

shine   shines, shiner, shined, shining, shiny, shone

ship ships, shipped, shipping, shipment, shipshape, shipyard

shirt shirts, shirtless

shock shocks, shocked, shocking, shockingly

shoe shoes, shoeing, shoeless, shod

shoot shoots, shooting, shot, shots

shop shops, shopper, shopped, shopping

shore shores

short shorter, shortest, shorten, shortish

should

shoulder shoulders, shouldered, shouldering

should not shouldn't

shout shouted, shouts, shouting

shove shoves, shoved, shoving

shovel shovels, shoveled, shoveling

show shows, showed, showing, showy, shown, show-off

shower showers, showered, showering, showery

shut shuts, shutting, shutter

sick sicker, sickest, sicken, sickish, sickened, sickening, sickness

side sides, sided, siding

sidewalk sidewalks

sigh sighs, sighed, sighing

sight sights, sighted, sighting, sightless, sightly

sign signs, signer, signed, signing, signature, signatures

signal signals, signaled, signaling

silent

silent silence, silenced, silencer, silencing, silently

silk silks, silky, silken

silly sillier, silliest, silliness

silver silvers, silvered, silvering, silvery

similar similarity, similarities, simile

simple simply, simpler, simplest, simplicity, simplify, simplifies, simplified, simplifying

since

sincere sincerely, sincerity, sincerest

sing sings, singing, sang, sung, singer

single singly, singular

sink sinks, sank, sinking, sunk, sinker, sunken

sir sirs

sister sisters, sister's

sit sitter, sitting, sat, sits

site sites

situate situates, situated, situating, situation, situations, situational

six sixth, sixths, sixteen, sixteens, sixteenths, sixty, sixties, sixtieth

size sizes, sized, sizing

skate skates, skater, skated, skating

skeleton skeletons

sketch sketches, sketcher, sketched, sketching, sketchy, sketchily, sketchiness

ski skis, skier, skied, skiing, skimobile

skid skids, skidded, skidding

skill skills, skilled, skillful, skillfully, skillfulness

skim skims, skimmer, skimmed, skimming

skin skins, skinned, skinny, skinless

skirt skirts, skirted, skirting

skit skits

skunk skunks, skunked, skunking

sky skies, skyline

slam slammed, slams, slamming

slave slaves, slaver, slaved, slaving, slavery, slavish

sleep sleeps, sleeper, sleepers, sleeping, slept

sleeve sleeves, sleeved

sleigh sleighs, sleighed, sleighing

slice slices, slicer, sliced, slicing

slide slid, slides, sliding, slider

slight slightly, slights, slighted, slighting, slightness

slip slips, slipper, slipping, slipped, slippery, slipperiness

slow slows, slower, slowed, slowing, slowest, slowly, slowness

slumber slumbers, slumbered, slumbering

small smaller, smallest, smallness, smallpox

smart smarter, smarten, smartest, smartly, smarty

smash smashed, smashes, smashing

smell smells, smeller, smelled, smelling, smelly, smellier, smelliest

smile smiles, smiled, smiling

smoke

smoke smokes, smoking, smoked

smooth smooths, smoothed, smoothing, smoothly, smoothness

smother smothers, smothered, smothering

snack snacks, snacked, snacking

snake snakes, snaked, snaky, snakiest

sneak sneaking, sneaks, sneaked, sneaker, sneakers

sneeze sneezed, sneezing, sneezes

snoop snooped, snooping, snoops, snoopy

snow snows, snowed, snowy, snowier, snowiest, snowing, snowfall

snowball snowballs, snowballing

so

soak soaks, soaker, soaked, soaking

soap soaps, soaped, soaping, soapy, soapier

soccer

social socially, sociable

society societies, societal

sock socks, socked, socking

soft softer, softest, softly, softness

soil soils, soiled, soiling

soldier soldiers, soldiering, soldierly

sole soles, solely

solid solidly, solidness

solo solos

solution solutions

solve solves, solved, solving, solvable, solver

some   somebody, somehow, someone, somewhat, somewhere, sometime, something, sometimes

somersault   somersaults, somersaulted, somersaulting

son   sons, sonny

song   songs

soon   sooner

sore   sores, sorer, sorest, soreness, sorely

sorrow   sorrows, sorrowed, sorrowing, sorrowful, sorrowfully

sorry

sort   sorts, sorted, sorting

soul   souls, soulful, soulfully, soulfulness, soulless

sound   sounds, sounded, sounding, soundly

soup   soups, soupy

sour   sours, soured, souring, sourly, sourer, sourest, sourness

source   sources

south   southern, southerly

space   spaces, spacer, spaced, spacing, spacious, spaciously, spaciousness

spade   spades, spaded, spading

spare   spares, spared, sparing

speak   speaks, speaker, speakers, speaking, speakable, spoke, spoken, speech, speeches, speechless

special   specialize, specializing, specialized, specially, specialist, specialty, especially

specimen   specimens

speed

speed   speeds, speeding, sped, speedier, speeded, speeder

spell   spells, spelled, speller, spelling

spend   spends, spender, spending, spent

spin   spins, spinner, spinning, spun

spirit   spirits, spirited, spiriting

spite   spites, spited, spiting, spiteful, spitefully, spitefulness

splash   splashes, splashed, splashing

splendid   splendidly

splendor   splendors

split   splits, splitter, splitting

spoil   spoils, spoiled, spoiling, spoilage

spook   spooky, spooks, spooking, spooked

sport   sports, sporting

spot   spots, spotter, spotted, spotting, spotty, spotless

spray   sprays, sprayed, sprayer, spraying

spread   spreads, spreader, spreading

spring   springs, springing, sprang, sprung, springtime

sprinkle   sprinkles, sprinkler, sprinkled, sprinkling

spy   spied, spies, spying

square   squares, squared, squaring, squarest, squareness

squash   squashes, squashed, squashing

squeeze   squeezes, squeezer, squeezed, squeezing

squirrel   squirrels, squirrelly

stable   stables, stabled

stack   stacks, stacked, stacking, stackful

staff   staffs, staffed, staffing

stair   stairs, stairway

stake   stakes, staked, staking

stalk   stalks, stalker, stalked, stalking

stamp   stamps, stamped, stamping

stand   stands, standing, stood

standard   standards, standardize, standardizing, standardization

star   stars, starred, starring

stare   stares, stared, staring

start   starts, starter, started, starting

startle   startled, startles, startling

starve   starves, starved, starver, starving, starvation

state   states, stated, stating, stately

station   stations, stationed, stationary

stationery   stationeries

statue   statues, statuary

stay   staying, stayed, stays

steady   steadies, steadied, steadiness, steadily, steadier, steadiest

steal   steals, stealing, stole, stolen

steam   steams, steamer, steamers, steaming, steamed, steamy

steel   steely

steep   steeper, steepest, steeply, steeped

steer

steer   steers, steered, steering, steerer, steerable, steerage

step   steps, stepped, stepping

stick   sticks, sticky, stuck, stickier

stiff   stiffen, stiffens, stiffened, stiffening, stiffness, stiffer, stiffest

still   stills, stilled, stillness

sting   stings, stinger, stinging, stung

stingy   stingily, stingier, stingiest, stinginess

stink   stank, stunk, stinking, stinks

stir   stirred, stirring, stirs

stitch   stitches, stitched, stitching

stocking   stockings

stomach   stomachs, stomach ache

stone   stones, stoned, stoning, stony

stoop   stoops, stooped, stooping

stop   stopped, stopping, stops

store   stores, storing, stored

storm   storms, stormy, stormiest, storming, stormed

story   stories, storybook, storyteller

stove   stoves

straight   straighten, straightening, straightened, straightener, straighter, straightest

strain   strains, strainer, strained, straining

strange   stranger, strangest, strangeness, strangely

strap   strapped, strapping, straps

straw

strawberry   strawberries

stray   strayed, straying, strays

stream   streams, streamed, streamer, streaming

street   streets, streetlight, streetcar

strength   strengthen, strengthened, strengthening

stretch   stretches, stretcher, stretched, stretching

strict   strictly, stricter, strictness, strictest

strike   stricken, striking, strikes, striker, struck

string   strings, stringing, strung, stringy

strip   strips, stripped, stripping, stripper

stroll   strolls, stroller, strolled, strolling

strong   stronger, strongest, strongly, strength

struggle   struggles, struggled, struggling, struggler

stubborn   stubbornly, stubbornness

study   studies, studied, studying, student, studious

stuff   stuffed, stuffing, stuffs

stump   stumps

stupid   stupidly, stupidity

style   styles, styled, styling, stylist, stylish, stylishly, stylishness

subject   subjects, subjected, subjecting

submarine   submarines

subscribe   subscribes, subscribing, subscribed, subscriber, subscription

substance

substance   substances, substantial,
  substantially

substitute   substitutes, substituted,
  substituting, substitution

succeed   succeeds, succeeded,
  succeeding, success, successful,
  successive, successor, succession

such

sudden   suddenly

suffer   suffers, suffered, suffering

sufficient   sufficiently

sugar   sugars, sugared, sugaring,
  sugary

suggest   suggests, suggested,
  suggesting, suggestion

suit   suits, suited, suiting, suitable,
  suitably

sum   sums, summary

summer   summery, summertime

sun   suns, sunned, sunning, sunny,
  sunset, sunrise

Sunday   Sun.

super   supercharge, superhighway,
  supermarket, superintendent

supper   suppers

supply   supplies, supplier, supplied,
  supplying

support   supports, supporter,
  supported, supporting

suppose   supposes, supposed,
  supposing, supposedly

supreme   supremely, supremacy

sure   surer, surest, surely

surface   surfaces, surfaced, surfacing

surgeon   surgeons, surgery, surgical

surprise   surprises, surprised, surprising, surprisingly

surrender   surrenders, surrendered, surrendering

surround   surrounds, surrounded, surrounding

survey   surveying, surveyed, surveys

suspect   suspects, suspected, suspecting, suspicion, suspicious, suspiciously

swamp   swamps, swampy, swamped, swamping

swan   swans

sway   sways, swayed, swaying

sweater   sweaters

sweep   sweeps, sweeper, sweeping, swept

sweet   sweets, sweeter, sweeten, sweetest, sweetener, sweetly

swell   swells, swelling, swelled, swollen

swift   swifter, swiftest, swiftly, swiftness

swim   swims, swam, swimmer, swimming, swum

swing   swinger, swinging, swung

switch   switches, switched, switching

sword   swords

syllable   syllables, syllabication

sympathy   sympathies, sympathetic, sympathetically, sympathize, sympathizes, sympathized, sympathizing, sympathizer

table

table tables, tablecloth

tablet tablets

tail tails, tailgate

take takes, taker, taken, taking, took

tale tales

talk talks, talker, talked, talking

tall taller, tallest, tallness

tame tames, tamed, taming, tamer, tamest

tank tanks

tariff tariffs

taste tastes, tasted, tasting, tasteless, tastelessly

tasty tastier, tastiest

tax taxes, taxing

taxi taxis, taxied, taxiing

tea teas, teaspoon, teaspoonful, teacup, teapot, teakettle

teach teaches, teacher, teaching, taught

team teams, teaming, teamed, teamster

tear tears, tearing, tore, torn

tease teases, teaser, teased, teasing, teasingly

telegram telegrams

telegraph telegraphs, telegraphed, telegraphing

telephone telephones, telephoning, telephoned

television televisions, televise, televising, televised

tell tells, teller, telling, told

temper   tempers, tempered, tempering

temperate   temperately, temperance

temperature   temperatures

temple   temples

ten   tenth

tend   tends, tender, tended, tending, tenderly, tenderness, tenderest

tennis

tent   tents, tenting, tented

term   terms, termed, terming

terrible   terribly, terribleness

territory   territories, territorial

terror   terrors, terrorism, terrorist, terrorize, terrorizes, terrorized, terrorizing

test   tests, tested, tester, testing

testimony   testimonies, testimonial, testify, testifying, testified

than

thank   thanks, thanking, thankful, thanked, Thanksgiving

that   that's

the

theater   theaters, theatrical

theft   thefts, thief, thieves, thievery, thieving

their   theirs

them   themselves, they, they're

then

theory   theories, theoretical

there   there's

thermometer

thermometer   thermometers

these   those

they   they're

thick   thicker, thickest, thickness, thickly

thin   thinly, thinner, thinned, thinning, thinnest

thing   things

think   thinks, thinker, thinking, thought, thoughtful

thirst   thirsts, thirsted, thirsting, thirsty

thirteen   thirteenth, thirty, thirtieth, third

this   that, these, those

thorough   thoroughly, thoroughness

though   although

thought   thoughtful, thoughtfully, thoughtfulness, thoughtless, thoughtlessly, thoughtlessness

thousand   thousands, thousandth

thread   threads, threaded, threading

three   third

thrill   thrills, thrilled, thrilling, thriller, thrillingly

throat   throats, throated

throne   thrones

through   throughout

throw   threw, throws, throwing, thrown, thrower

thumb   thumbs, thumbed, thumbing, thumbtack

thunder   thundering, thundered, thunders, thunderstorm

Thursday   Thurs.

ticket   tickets, ticketed, ticketing

tickle   tickles, tickled, tickling, ticklish

tie   ties, tied, tying

tiger   tigress

tight   tights, tighter, tightest, tighten, tightens, tightened, tightly, tightness, taut

tile   tiles, tiled, tiling

time   times, timed, timing

timid   timidly, timidness

tinker   tinkers, tinkered, tinkering

tiny   tinier, tiniest

tip   tips, tipped, tipping

tire   tires, tired, tiring, tiredness, tiresome, tireless, tirelessly, tirelessness

to

toad   toads, toadstool

tobacco   tobaccos, tobacconist

today

together   togetherness

tomorrow

tone   tones, toned, toning, toner, toneless

tongue   tongues, tongued

tonight

too

tool   tools, tooling, toolbox

tooth   teeth

top   tops, topped, topping

topic   topics, topical, topically

torment   torments, tormented, tormenting, tormentor

torrid   torridly

toss   tosses, tosser, tossed, tossing

total   totals, totaled, totaling, totally

touch   touching, touched, touches, touchdown

tough   tougher, toughest, toughly, toughness, toughen, toughened, toughening

tour   tours, touring, toured, tourist, tourism

tournament   tournaments, tourney

toward   towards

towel   towels, toweling

tower   towers, towered, towering

town   towns, township, townsman

toy   toys

trace   traces, tracer, traced, tracing

track   tracks, tracker, tracked, tracking, trackless

tractor   tractors

trade   trades, trader, traded, trading

traffic   trafficked, trafficking, trafficker

trail   trails, trailer, trailed, trailing

train   trainer, trained, trains, training

transport   transports, transported, transporting, transportation

trap   traps, trapper, trapped, trapping

trash   trashy

travel   travels, traveler, traveled, traveling

treasure   treasurer, treasuries, treasury

treat   treats, treated, treating, treatment, treatments

tree   trees, treed, treeing

tremendous   tremendously

tribe   tribes, tribesman

trick   tricks, tricked, tricking, tricky, trickster

trim   trims, trimmer, trimmed, trimming

trip   trips, tripped, tripping

triumph   triumphs, triumphed, triumphing, triumphant, triumphantly

troll   trolls, trolling, trolled

troop   troops, trooper, trooped, trooping

trophy   trophies

trot   trotting, trotted, trots, trotter

trouble   troubles, troubled, troubling, troublesome, troublemaker

trousers

trout

truck   trucks, trucked, trucking

true   truer, truly, truth, truthful, truthfully, truthfulness

trumpet   trumpets, trumpeted, trumpeting, trumpeter

trunk   trunks, trunkful

trust   trusts, trusted, trusty, trusting, truth, trustee, trustworthy

try   tries, tried, trying, tryout, trial

tub   tubs, tubby, tubful

Tuesday   Tues.

tulip   tulips

tunnel   tunnels, tunneled, tunneling

turkey   turkeys

turn   turns, turned, turning

turtle   turtles, turtleneck

twelve   twelves, twelfth

twenty   twenties, twentieth, twenty-five, twenty-fives, twenty-fifth

twice

twilight   twilights

twin   twins

twist   twists, twister, twisted, twisting

two

type   types, typed, typing

typewriter   typewrites, typewritten, typewriting

typhoid

ugly   uglier, ugliest, ugliness

umpire   umpires, umpired, umpiring

unable   inability

uncertain   uncertainly, uncertainty, certain

uncle   uncles

uncomfortable   uncomfortably

uncommon   uncommonly, uncommonness

unconscious   unconsciously,
  unconsciousness, conscious

under   underneath, underwater,
  underground

underdog

understand   understood,
  understanding, understands

underwear

undone   undid, undoing

undress   undresses, undressed,
  undressing

uneasy   uneasily, uneasiness,
  uneasier, uneasiest, easy

unexpected   unexpectedly, expect

unfortunate   unfortunately, fortune,
  fortunately

unhappy   unhappier, unhappiest,
  happy

uniform   uniforms, uniformed,
  uniformly

union   unions

unite   unites, united, uniting

United States   U.S.

university   universities

unjust   unjustly

unknown   unknowing, know

unless

unload   unloads, unloaded, unloading

unlock   unlocks, unlocked, unlocking

unnecessary   unnecessarily,
  necessary

unpack   unpacks, unpacked,
  unpacking, pack

unpleasant unpleasantly, unpleasantness, unpleasing, pleasant

until till

unusual unusually, usual

unwise unwisely, wise

up upper

upon

upstairs

urge urges, urged, urging, urgency, urgent, urgently

us

use uses, used, user, using, useful, usefully, usefulness, useless, uselessness

usher ushers, ushered, ushering

usual usually

utmost uttermost

utter utters, uttered, uttering, utterance, utterer, utterable, utterly, uttermost, utmost

vacant vacancy, vacantly

vacation vacations, vacationer, vacationers, vacationed, vacationing

vain vainly, vanity

valentine valentines, Valentine's Day

valley valleys

value values, valued, valuing, valuable, valueless

vampire vampires

vanish   vanishes, vanished, vanishing

vary   varies, varied, varying, various, variously, variety, varieties, variation

vast   vaster, vastest, vastly, vastness

vegetable   vegetables

vegetate   vegetates, vegetated, vegetating, vegetation

velvet   velvets, velvety

venture   ventures, ventured, venturer, venturing

vertical   vertically

very

vessel   vessels

veterinarian   veterinarians, veterinary

vice   vices

vicinity   vicinities

victim   victims, victimize, victimizes, victimized, victimizing

victory   victories, victorious, victoriously, victor

view   views, viewer, viewed, viewing

village   villages, villager

vinegar

violent   violence, violently

violet   violets

visible   visibly, visibility

visit   visits, visited, visiting, visitor, visitors

vocation   vocations, vocational, vocationally

voice   voices, voiced, voicing, voiceless

volcano

volcano volcanoes, volcanic, vulcanism

voluntary voluntarily, volunteer, volunteered, volunteering

vote votes, voting, voted, voter

voyage voyages, voyaged, voyaging, voyager

vulgar vulgarly, vulgarity

wade wades, waded, wader, wading

wagon wagons, wagonload

waist waists, waistband

wait waits, waiter, waited, waiting

wake woke, wakes, wakeful, waken, waking

walk walks, walker, walked, walking

wall walls, walled

wand wands

wander wanders, wanderer, wandered, wandering

want wanted, wants, wanting

war wars, warred, warring, warlike, warrior

ward wards, warden

warehouse warehouses

warm warmed, warming, warms

warn warned, warning, warns

was was not, wasn't

wash washes, washer, washed, washing, washers

Washington

waste   wastes, waster, wasted, wasting, wasteful, wastefully

watch   watches, watcher, watched, watching

water   waters, waterer, watered, watering, waterless, watermelon

wave   waves, waved, waving

way   ways

we   we're, we'll, we'd

weak   weaker, weakest, weakly

wealth   wealthy, wealthier, wealthiest

wear   wears, wearer, wearing, wore, worn

weary   wearies, wearied, wearier, wearying, wearily, weariness

weather   weathered, weatherproof, weathers, weathering

weave   weaves, weaver, weaving, wove, woven

wed   wedding, weddings

Wednesday   Wed.

wee

weed   weeds, weeded, weedy, weeding

week   weeks   weekend   weekends

weigh   weighed, weighing, weight, weights, weighted, weightless, weighty

weird   weirder, weirdest, weirdly

welcome   welcomes, welcomed, welcoming

well   wells

went

were   were not, weren't

west   western, westerly

wet   wets, wetting, wetter, wettest

whale   whales, whaling, whaled,
whaler, whaleboat, whalebone

what   what's

wheat   wheats

wheel   wheels, wheeled, wheeling

when

where

whether

which

while

whimper   whimpers, whimpering,
whimpered

whisper   whispered, whispering,
whispers

white

whiz   whizzed, whizzing, whizzes

who   whom, whose, whoever, who's

whole   wholes, wholesome

why

wide   wider, widest, widely, width,
wideness, widen, widened

wife   wives

wiggle   wiggles, wiggled, wiggling,
wiggly

wild   wilder, wildest, wilderness, wildly

will   wills, willed, willing, would, willful,
will not, won't

willow   willows

win   wins, winner, winning, won

wind   winds, windy, windier, windiest

wind   winds, winding, wound

window   windows, windowpane, windowsill

windshield   windshields

wine   wines, winery, wined

wing   wings, winged, winging, wingless

winter   winters, wintering, wintery

wire   wires, wired, wiring, wiry, wirelike

wise   wiser, wisest, wisely, wisdom

wish   wishes, wished, wishing

witch   witches, witchcraft

with

wither   withers, withered, withering

within   without

witness   witnesses, witnessed, witnessing

wolf   wolves, wolfed, wolfing, wolfish

woman   women, womanly

wonder   wonders, wondered, wondering, wonderful, wonderfully, wondrous

wood   woods, wooden, wooded, woodiness, woody

wool   woolen, wooly

word   words, worded, wording, wordy, wordless

work   works, worked, working, worker

world   worlds, worldly, worldliness

worm

worm worms, wormed, worming, wormy, wormier, wormiest

worry worries, worried, worrying, worriedly

worse worst, worsen, worsened, worsening

worth worthy, worthiness, worthless, worthlessness

would would not, wouldn't

wound wounds, wounded, wounding

wrap wraps, wrapper, wrapped, wrapping

wrench wrenches, wrenched, wrenching

wrestle wrestles, wrestling, wrestled, wrestler

write writes, writer, writing, wrote, written

wrong wrongs, wronged, wronging, wrongly

yard yards, yardage, yardstick

year years, yearly, yearbook

yeast

yell yells, yelled, yelling

yellow

yes

yesterday

yet

yield yields, yielded, yielding, yielder, yieldingly

you   yourself, yourselves, your, you'll,
you've, yours, you'd, you're

youth   youths, youthful, youthfully,
youthfulness, young

zebra

zero   zeros, zeroes, zeroed, zeroing

zip   zips, zipped, zipping, zipper

zone   zoned, zoning, zones

zoo   zoos, zoology

zoom   zoomed, zooms, zooming

ADDITIONAL WORDS

ADDITIONAL WORDS